First
Hour

Very early in the morning, while it was still dark,

Jesus got up, left the house and went off to a

Solitary place where he prayed.

Mark 1:35

The
First
Hour
for Men

Presented To:

_____

From:

_____

Date:

_____

The Mission

To train men to become everything God intended

Them to be...Godly Men—Fathers—Leaders;

Equipping them to spread the message of

Jesus Christ throughout the world.

SEARCHED... FED... LED!

The first hour of every day has been the most meaningful, challenging, yet the most glorious Hour of my day for the past 40 years. The first thing I do every morning is fall to my knees in Prayer and repentance. We sin everyday, hence I start my day in prayer reflecting on the past 24 hours so that I can confess what needs to be confessed. What a joy it is to know that His forgiveness is guaranteed. After prayer, I read the Word of God. Once I have done this, I am a vessel ready to be led by the Spirit. My first hour is meaningful because I meet with God, it is challenging because the Word of God will convict me when I have missed the mark, and it is glorious because of His forgiveness and the confident assurance that I will be led each day by His Spirit. I endorse and recommend wholeheartedly *The First Hour for Men*, as it is precisely what I have been doing for many years.

Coach Bill McCartney
Founder, Promise Keepers

I spent 20 years in the Army living each day in strict obedience to the Army regulation. I did well in the Army as a direct result of my obedience to the Army regulation. I gave my life to Jesus my last year in the military and realized immediately that I had a new regulation – The Bible. I immediately began to live my life in strict adherence to the Word of God in the same way that I obeyed the Army regulation. My spiritual maturity increased rapidly. Then I met Coach Mac, a man of prayer, who would not answer a question without asking for divine guidance. It revolutionized my life. For the last 20 years, as direct result of Coach's influence on my life, my first hour of every day is governed by being Searched, Fed and Led by the Spirit. *"The First Hour for Men Study Guide is truly God's tool that will transform and equip men to be Godly men who are daily led by the Spirit of the Living God."*

Raleigh B. Washington, DD, M. Div
President/CEO, Promise Keepers

Foreword *by* Rich DeVos

It's not easy for many men to humble themselves before God. We've been brought up to be tough on the playing fields, not to cry, to be heads of households, bread winners and hard-nosed businessmen. We don't like stopping for directions, let alone asking someone for help.

We pride ourselves on being self-made, but we're really God-made. He knows our hearts better than we know ourselves. And only God knows the plan He has for our lives. So why wouldn't we naturally turn to our Father in Heaven to ask for guidance?

The First Hour makes it simple. Just one hour a day that will change your life and help you to seek God first.

I've built very successful businesses, so some people might view me as self-sufficient and in control. But I realize everything I have and everything I am is by the grace of God. So, before tackling business and facing the demands of the day, I face God. It is there, without distraction, where, as a husband, as a father and as a man, I can appreciate all the blessings I've been given and evaluate the ways in which I'm using those gifts.

In these pages Mark gives all men a step-by-step outline to spending a fulfilling hour a day with God. From spiritual enlightenment, to career development, to strengthening their marriage, to their own self worth, there isn't a fundamental area of a man's life that cannot be improved by following this 30-day study guide.

Richard M. DeVos, Sr.
Co-Founder, Amway Corporation

The First Hour Mission
"Restoring God's America"

America is at a crossroads. For the last 100 years our traditional Judeo/Christian values have been slowly and methodically eroded to the point that our founding fathers vision for "One Nation Under God" is hardly recognizable. Prayer has been removed from our schools, the Ten Commandments have been removed from our courtrooms and most importantly God has been removed as the head of our households. We are on a rapid descent into a Godless society where massive Government replaces spirituality in the lives of everyday Americans.

However, we believe that the main reason for this moral decay, is because "We The People" have veered away from the Godly principles this country was founded on.

It's America's men that have lost their own integrity and morals throughout the decades and have set an ungodly, poor example, to their children and families. In order to turn this country around and begin the process of healing this Nation, we must first turn its men around and begin to heal them.

The First Hour for men is a simple, effective tool that is making a major impact in the process of restoring America back to "One Nation Under God."

The First Hour is uniting Godly men in America to become prayer warriors that are committing to changing themselves, their family and ultimately this nation through prayer and a pledge to their patriotic duty. We believe:

If You Heal The Man... He Will Heal His Family...
The Family Will Heal The Nation!

1. Heal the Man

We must first bring America's men back to a closer "Daily Relationship" with God. The evil forces that are destroying this Nation are a direct result of men, the head of the household, living in disobedience and ignoring God's Commandments. Without the men in this country first changing themselves, the family does not stand a chance and America is destined for continual destruction.

"The First Hour" for men, is accomplishing the goal of restoring the man back to a closer daily relationship with God. Our goal is to distribute One Million copies throughout the U.S. over the next several years. To date, over 100,000 books have been shipped to men across the Nation. Why One Million? We need at least one million men to be a tipping point for change.

We encourage these men to make three commitments.

First - Commit to completing the 30-day study. Numerous testimonies are coming in and miracles of restoration are happening in the lives of men and their families who are committing to and completing this 30-day study.

Second - Commit to all 7 steps of the First Hour process, which can result in dramatic changes in all areas of their life.

Third - Commit to share this book with five other men. Each man will commit to give away five books, two books to fellow believers to keep the momentum going, and three books to men that they believe do not have a personal relationship with Jesus Christ. This will continue to create a grass roots "MLM" type movement throughout the nation and inspire a movement of the Holy Spirit that we believe will make a difference for generations to come.

2. Heal the Family

Once the Man turns back to a solid daily relationship with God and returns to his role as the spiritual head of the household, he will then consciously and unconsciously begin to heal his family by providing a positive, Godly example. The First Hour is assisting in this process by providing them with the tools and educational materials to begin to restore their family. The restoration of the American family is the key to restoring our founding father's dream of a government that is "Of the People, By the People and For the People," under the direction of God.

3. Heal the Nation

With millions of men praying every morning, we can begin the process of changing this Nation back into the God-fearing, traditional value system that our founding fathers designed.

The final step to continue the process of healing this Nation is to get all the First Hour partners and their families to make a "Solid Commitment" to their "Patriotic Duty" and vote. We will call on them to Vote in every single election from here on out. From the county school boards, to the local judges, the mayor, the governor and every single local, state and National election. No matter what their political party affiliation, they must vote for the candidates who respect the Constitution and the Godly Principles upon which this great Nation was founded on.

We will encourage and challenge every man in this Nation to get back to a closer daily relationship with God. We will challenge them to become the spiritual leader of their homes, we will challenge them to become the man, the father and the husband that God intended them to be. We will challenge them to rise up and vote for the Godly politicians that share the same moral principals and values that they do.

And lastly, we will challenge them to share the message of salvation through a personal relationship with Jesus Christ. We all need to join together and do our part in the Great Commission to help heal this nation. United in God we stand, divided from Him we fall. With Gods help and our commitment, America can return to "One Nation Under God."

God Bless You...And God Bless America!

Mark W. Koch

The First Hour
The story behind the study

You are about to begin what I believe will be the best thirty days you will ever experience in your life. It's no coincidence that you have this book in your hands right now. There is no doubt in my mind that this is a Divine appointment between <u>you and God!</u>

As you read how The First Hour began, I hope you will be convinced that I had nothing to do with the creation of this study guide. This is God's message to you; it was developed by Him, not me. I truly believe that I was just chosen to put it on paper for you. I know that's a pretty bold statement; it might even sound arrogant, but believe me, God has humbled me many times over. So, what I am trying to say is this devotion is a gift from God to YOU, and I take no credit for it. My background is pretty simple. I had a dream, pursued it, and accomplished it. I was a big shot Hollywood producer, or so I thought. I broke some box office records with my film *Lost in Space*, made a lot of money, achieved all of my worldly dreams, was at the top of my game, and was totally miserable. With a broken marriage, an ego the size of Manhattan and truly "lost in space", I cried out to God. He answered, stripped me down to nothing, took all my worldly possessions, remolded me, and lifted me back up, but this time for His glory. So here's how the story goes. It may seem far-fetched to you, maybe a bit crazy, or just a series of coincidences, but I challenge you to seek God with the same passion that I did, ask Him to give you signs for yourself, and then make your determination. I believe He <u>will</u> answer you in the same way He did me.

First of all, I want you to understand how God revealed all the information for me to write down in this study. God speaks to people in many different ways. It is very common for people to say that God spoke to my spirit, God spoke to my heart, or God spoke to me in a dream. God spoke to me in a very simple way; He spoke to my mind. I am convinced that He made my thoughts agreeable to His will. The ideas that would come into my mind to write down for this course would just come out of nowhere. I had no premeditated plan to develop a study guide for men. In fact, I had no desire to do this at all. I am convinced that the Holy Spirit guided me through each simple step for me to share with you. You are truly blessed, because God has chosen you to get to know Him more intimately through these next thirty days. Your life is about to change...drastically!

Early one morning in July of 2004, I woke up suddenly, rolled over in bed, and looked at my alarm clock. The bright digital numbers read 5:55 a.m. I didn't have a bad dream or hear any loud noise. The reason this was so unusual was because I am not a morning person; I never have been one of those people that can get out of bed early in the morning. I have always been a night owl, working until at least midnight and most of the time into the wee hours of the night. It was God who woke me up at 5:55 a.m. that morning. As I looked at the clock and laid back down to go to sleep, over and over in my mind the same thought kept agonizing me, "Give God your first waking hour every morning for the next thirty days; a half hour of prayer and a half hour of reading His Word." The thought kept racing through my mind! Get up, go pray, and read the Bible. I kept fighting it, trying to go back to sleep, but I was wide- awake. God allowed me no choice in the matter. I felt the presence of the Holy Spirit like I have never felt before. Two things just kept repeating themselves over and over in my mind... get up and go pray for a half hour, and read the Bible for a half hour. Give God the first hour of every day for the next thirty days. I could not even think about anything else. Finally, I got out of bed and went upstairs to pray. I kept saying to myself, thirty minutes of prayer? What was I going to pray about for thirty minutes? I can pretty much ask God for everything I need in five minutes or less. I went upstairs to my desk and sat down. I kept thinking to myself, thirty minutes of prayer, that's a long time!

As I sat down at my desk, right smack in the middle of it was the book, *Prayers That Avail Much* by Germaine Copeland. It was given to my wife as a birthday gift from her friend; she must have put it on my desk knowing I was the one that needed the prayers. "Perfect!" I said to myself. "I will just go through the contents page and pick out some prayers that I feel pertain to me and my needs and start praying as many of them as I can until thirty minutes is up." That's exactly what I did. I went through the table of contents and started to pick prayers randomly. I was going from prayers on page 174 to page 42 back to page 257 to page 72 and so on. I had no particular order. I thought I was just choosing the prayers that just came into my mind. What I didn't realize at the time was that God had a plan. He was leading me in a particular order.

After thirty minutes sharp, I stopped and picked up my Bible. I knew that God wanted me to read a half hour of His Word. What part of the Bible should I read for thirty minutes? What came to my mind instantly was the book of Proverbs and The New Testament. The book of Proverbs was perfect because there are 31 chapters, and I had committed to 30 days. Each chapter was approximately a page to a page and a half, and would only take a couple of minutes. The next thing I did was look in my Bible and see how many pages were in the New Testament— there were two hundred and forty in my NIV version. Two hundred and forty divided by thirty days was only 8 pages a day. I said to myself, "If I only read 4 pages a day front and back, I would have read the entire New Testament in 30 days." The next thing God revealed to me was that I was to learn The Ten Commandments … inside out… upside down … and from the middle! When I finished, I had five minutes left over. I then asked God what to do with the last five minutes, and what instantly came to my mind was close your eyes and listen to Me.

To make sure I read the prayers in the same order each day, I attached yellow sticky notes the very first day and numbered the order of the prayers. After the first week, I was getting tired of jumping around from all the different pages in the book, and the sticky notes were starting to fall off, so I decided to have my assistant type up the prayers in the order that I was praying them each day. When she finished retyping them, she printed them out and handed them to me. She looked as white as a ghost. She said, "Do you see what I see? It's what my Pastor always says, God first, family second, career third." I looked through the freshly typed sheets, and sure enough, the first several prayers all pertained to God, the second set pertained to family, and the third pertained to career. I did not plan this. I believe this is a message from God to you on how He wants you to set your priorities in life. They were in perfect order. As you know, our God is a God of perfect order. It is not a coincidence that the order just happened to come out that way. I can assure you that this was truly Divine intervention.

After the first couple of days, I asked my wife if she would make up a 30-day chart on her computer for me to check off my assignments. The second she handed me the chart, I immediately wrote down seven things that I wanted to accomplish in the 30-day period. There was no thought about it. It was automatic… the seven steps just came to my mind and flew through me. I just recently learned that the number seven is a very important Biblical number, it Means COMPLETION!

By the end of the third week, people were noticing a drastic change in me; they noticed a certain peace about me that they had not seen before. They began asking me what I was doing differently. I just had to share it. I was getting up at 5:55 every morning and giving my First Hour to God, and I'd never felt this great in my entire life. My assistant came to me and said, "You need to put this in a simple course for everyone who is asking what you are doing." She wanted her husband to start it immediately.

I spent the next two days in my office putting the 30-day program together for a few friends. I never understood why I was driven to make it so clear and important that they should memorize the Ten Commandments for ten days straight and then write them over and over again until they were hammered into their heads. It was so elementary. I mean after the first ten days of repeating them, a first grader could have memorized them. As you read on, you will see the significance of this.

Throughout the next several months, I still had no intention of making this a book to be available to the general public. It was something that I put together only to share with a few of my friends, not realizing that God had other plans. This is when God confirmed to me, in his own way, that He had other plans to bring this material to the world. It was almost comical. Everywhere I looked, the number 555 came up. For the next several months, at least once or twice a week, 555 appeared to me in the craziest places. Here are just a few of the examples.

Numerous times after I finished my first hour with God, I turned the television on and as soon as I turned it on, I heard the Domino's 555 commercial. "555 just 555. Three pizzas for just $5.55 each." I saw this ad everywhere, on Billboards, newspapers, I heard it on the radio over and over. It was a huge campaign for them and it hounded me for months.

I went to the doctor to schedule my eye surgery. They gave me the date: April 27, 2005. They called me on April 24th and told me they were going to have to reschedule my appointment for the following week. On May 5th, the day of my appointment, I showed up for my surgery. As they handed me the fifteen different release documents to sign, each time I signed my name, I had to date it. As I dated the very first signature, I realized... here we go again, May 5, 2005, which of course, I abbreviated, 05-05-05. I just laughed, but I was starting to understand that God had a message for me regarding the 555. It was getting ridiculous. It was way beyond coincidental. My airline flight that I have been taking to L.A. for 6 years always departed at 6:15. They changed it to 5:55. I took my wife's car into Firestone to get new tires, on the work order they put 555 in two separate places. Under the license number it said 555-FL and under mileage they put 555 miles. Obviously that is not her tag number or the mileage of the car. He was probably just too busy to go check the tag and mileage. I kept the work order and will frame it as a reminder. I could go on and on as to how many times the numbers appeared to me, but I don't want to bore you. However, I do have to give you one more example that put the icing on the cake for me.

I was in Miami at a delicatessen and I sat down to have lunch by myself. I ordered a turkey sandwich and a bottle of water, even though I really wanted a Mountain Dew. I'd been trying to change my drinking habits. When my turkey sandwich arrived, I bowed my head to pray. With so many different things going on in my life at this particular time, my prayer was very simple. "Lord, it seems that I'm going in so many directions right now. Please show me your will for my life and reveal to me what you want me to focus my time on." At least, three separate times during lunch, the waitress passed me with a can of Mountain Dew, delivering each of them to other customers. Finally, the pressure was too much. I caved in. I was down to the last couple of bites of my sandwich and I waved the waitress over. I told her that I couldn't stand it any longer! "Bring me a can of Mountain Dew!" She laughed and brought me the Mountain Dew. She also picked my bill up and recalculated it, adding the 90 cents more for the Mountain Dew. What do you suppose the bill came out to then? Five dollars and fifty-five cents—$5.55! I said, "OK Lord. I get it. I will focus on this 30-Day Study for men."

During the same time as all of the 555 messages, the Ten Commandments also kept popping up everywhere. Judge Roy Moore just happened to be in the news at the time that I was designing the pages for the study to give to friends. Out of the blue, he called me personally and asked me to get involved in his fight to help him keep the country's focus on the laws of the founding Fathers of our nation, specifically, The Ten Commandments. He was ordered to remove The Ten Commandments monument from the State Supreme Court building. It was all over the news channels and press for several weeks. He wanted me to make a movie about it. A few days later I had a project offered to me to do a remake of the film "The Decalogue." I didn't even know what that word meant. When I asked my partner about it, he told me it was a project about the Ten Commandments. When I went to church that Sunday, my pastor announced that over the next ten weeks he would be doing a study on… you guessed it… the Ten Commandments. Again, I could go on and on, just as I was hounded by the 555 message, I was equally hounded by signs of the Ten Commandments. I think you get the message of what God was trying to get through my thick skull here. He wanted to make sure I would include the Commandments in this course and reveal to you how important they are to Him. After all, they are His laws.

I got the message, came up with the title *Tender Warriors 5:55*, designed the book and printed up five hundred of them. As you begin this study, and read through the prayers, you will see that the sixth prayer that I have been praying for a couple of months during this time was, "To Walk in God's Wisdom and His Perfect Will." The first sentence says, "Father, I ask You to give me a complete understanding of what You want to do in my life…" and it goes on later to say, "I roll my works upon You, Lord, and You make my thoughts agreeable to Your will…" All of these revelations of the 555 shouldn't be such a surprise to me… or to you. After all, I'd been praying every morning for several months for God to reveal His will for my life. God always answers the prayers of those who diligently seek Him, and I know as you begin your journey of giving your *First Hour* to God, He will reveal His will for your life as well. Don't be surprised if the number 555 starts popping up all over the place. It has happened to many men who have started this course.

Finally, after these books started circulating to all of my friends, the meaning of 555 was revealed to me. A good friend of mine, Dean Lovett, came to my office. As soon as he picked up the book and looked at the title, he questioned me on the number 555 and what the meaning of that was. I explained to him all the 555 messages God has hounded me with and that I was convinced it was the time he wanted me and YOU to get up each morning and spend the *First Hour* with Him. He said, "Mark, everyone is not going to get up at 5:55. That couldn't have been His purpose. There has to be some other reason for it." He asked me if I had gone through The Bible and found any Scripture that is relevant with those numbers involved. I told him I had researched it extensively and that there is no chapter 5, verse 55 in any of the books. He left my office and headed home.

He was so troubled by it, that he was completely driven to figure it out.

He searched the entire Bible, trying to figure out if there was another reason besides getting up at 5:55 in the morning for this number. He was so bothered by it that he actually pulled over to the side of the road after leaving my office and frantically searched his Bible. He was getting ready to close the book because he couldn't find it anywhere. Then God spoke to him. What instantly came into his mind was to check the 5th book, 5th chapter and 5th verse. He went to the fifth book, which is Deuteronomy and went to the fifth chapter; the heading was in bold black and said: "THE TEN COMMANDMENTS." He then went to the fifth verse, which by the way is in parentheses, and says: "AT THAT TIME I stood between the Lord and you to declare to you the word of the Lord." Dean called me on the phone, barely able to talk, and said, " Go get your Bible and go to Deuteronomy, which is the fifth book, go to the fifth chapter and read the fifth verse." When I looked it up, chills ran through my body. I finally had the answer to what 555 meant. It means, "I am standing between God and you to reconfirm His message to you." It's all about the Ten Commandments. These are His laws, His rules.

As I continued to pray the prayers each morning and spend time with God for the next several months, something else very important was revealed to me. Besides the Ten Commandments, there is another message that I believe God gave to me to share with you. *The three key factors to effective and powerful prayer.* Again, there is no coincidence that these are the first three prayers in the prayer section of the book. Here they are:

The first thing you must do is put on the Armor of God each morning.
"God is strong, and He wants you strong. So take everything the Master has set out for you, well-made weapons of the best materials, and put them to use so you will be able to stand up to everything the devil throws your way." - Ephesians 6:10-11 (MESSAGE)

Start out each morning with the simple first prayer included in this study "To Put on the Armor of God." This will protect your mind from all the enemy's distractions.

Although we seldom realize it, we're always wrestling against the unseen powers in the spiritual realm. There's an unending struggle and prayer is the weapon that will turn the tide. "Watch out for your great enemy, the devil. He prowls around like a roaring lion, looking for someone to devour." - 1 Peter 5:8 (NLT)

Satan will do whatever he can to keep you from praying and communicating with God, because he knows you are completely helpless against him on your own. But when we approach the devil on **praying ground**, in the mighty strength of the Lord, we stand in a strength that's superior to the devil in every way. He wants to keep that weapon out of our hands!

It's interesting that God's Word compares the devil to a lion. When a lion catches its prey, it will often use its powerful jaws to clamp down on the mouth of its unfortunate victim. It does this so its prey can't cry out for help from the rest of its herd. That's Satan's strategy against us. He wants to keep us quiet, to keep us from prayer, because he knows the armies of heaven are at our call.

The second thing you must do is pray for forgiveness and repentance.
God's ears are closed to an unclean heart and spirit. You must first ask God to forgive you for all of the sins from the previous day (don't we all have some), and you must truly repent and ask God to forgive you. What God was revealing to me was that He will hear our prayers, but He will not listen to them or answer them unless we pray to Him with a freshly renewed and clean spirit. I did some research on this and sure enough, this is what I found in the Bible:

"It's your sins that have cut you off from God. Because of your sins, He has turned away and will not listen anymore." - Isaiah 59:2 (NLT)

Why should we bother confessing our sins to God when we pray?" Isaiah's words should send a chill up our spines, "Because of your sins, He has turned away and will not listen anymore."

Sin... unconfessed sin... has a way of dulling God's ears to our prayers!

When there's something wicked and sinful buried in our hearts, God doesn't pretend that everything is OK. He is determined that we deal with it before moving forward with the plans He has for us.

When we ask God to forgive us and cover our sins with the Blood of Jesus Christ and we truly mean it, all of our sins are forgiven. At that moment, our spirit is clean before the eyes of the Lord. It may only last for one hour, or for some of us maybe only five minutes after our time spent with Him, but at that moment, each morning, we are without sin in His eyes. What a gift of grace. "For the eyes of the Lord are upon the righteous, those who are upright and in right standing with God, and His ears are attentive (open) to their prayer." -1 Peter 3:12

The third thing you must do, is ask for a fresh refilling of the Holy Spirit.
Jesus said, "How much more shall your Heavenly Father give the Holy Spirit to those who ask Him." - Luke 11:13b and Acts 1:8 says "But you will receive power when the Holy Spirit comes on you."

You now have the secret to effective and powerful prayer; it's as simple as one, two, three! Put on your armor; ask Him for forgiveness, pray for a fresh refilling of the Holy Spirit, and you are now ready to approach the throne of the Almighty God.

God has a plan for your life. He's your Father and you're His son. He wants a father and son relationship with you, He wants you to be successful, He can't help you unless you let Him. He will discipline you, He will ground you. He will also lift you up. However, you need to follow His rules. You have to strive for obedience!

Obedience = Blessings... Disobedience = Discipline... it's that simple!

As I was writing this letter to you, many times I tried to dig into Scripture and make this as intelligent as I could. Yet the more I tried to add Scripture and stories from the Bible to try to validate my message to you, the more I would just get discouraged and end up back at square one. I would always go back to just writing from the heart, writing from what I truly believe was coming from God, not me. The message that God kept putting into my mind was K.I.S.S. "Keep it simple Son." I am not a theologian, nor am I a Bible scholar. As a matter of fact, most of you reading this right now probably know Scripture a lot better than I do. The reason I believe that God has chosen me is because I am one of His children that is just an average "C" student at best. Therefore, the message is simple.

I will not try to teach you anything. God will reveal everything He wants you to know over the next thirty days with Him. I believe I was just chosen to share with you the three simple steps to effective prayer and a life' changing experience when you earnestly seek and spend quality time with Him and follow His commandments.

Remember, NOT ONE OF US is without sin. Not your pastor, not your earthly father, not your mentor, not even the Pope is without sin. Let's face up, let's get serious; we were born in sin and our minds are not pure. But I believe a Godly man is the man that strives to be righteous on a daily basis, a man that fights it with all his heart, and when he falls into sin, he gets back up, repents and gives it another shot. A true man falls, gets back up and keeps on trying. If we can leave this world with 80% of our flesh dead, I believe that is a true success. None of us will ever be as pure as Jesus, though some of us want others to believe we are. Get up each morning and fight the good fight, avoid sin with all you have, and when you fall into it, repent from it, ask for forgiveness and move on. God knows your heart, but He also knows your weaknesses.

In Conclusion, this book gives you the opportunity to start fresh every day. It gives you the chance to really get to know your Heavenly Father and have a true relationship with Him. It gives you the opportunity to be all that He wants you to be and experience the life He has planned for you. He has a destiny for you, and a perfect plan for your life. Spend time with Him each day, pray to Him, love Him, seek Him, and ask Him to help you to be the son He wants you to be. Strive for obedience, and watch Him change, mold, and use you in a way you could have never imagined. He loves you. LOVE HIM! Talk to Your Father each and every morning until you finally meet Him face to face.

The time is now! Get up tomorrow morning and begin your new journey and watch the blessings start pouring in. I know that God will show you the same thing that He showed me as you start your first hour each morning with Him. The prayers in this study are powerful and will change you from the inside out. They will reveal God's will for you, guide you through each day, and affect every area of your life.

May God Bless you abundantly,
Mark W. Koch

The First Hour Commitment

I truly believe that The First Hour for men is a gift from God to you. It's now in your hands and I ask that you make the following three commitments below. If you are not ready at this time to commit to this program, please pass this book on to someone you feel could benefit by committing to this 30-day study.

COMMITMENT 1

I commit to giving God my first hour each morning for the next thirty days by completing "The First Hour" study guide.

COMMITMENT 2

I commit to follow all of the seven simple steps (on page 18) that make up the *First Hour* 30 day program.

COMMITMENT 3

I commit to doing my part in "The Great Commission" by sharing *The First Hour for Men* study guide with **five** other men; **two** fellow Christian brothers and **three** men that I feel do not have a personal relationship with Jesus Christ.

I hereby agree to keep the three commitments above.

_____

Signature

The First Hour
Objectives

By the end of this 30 day study, and by prayerfully seeking God as you dedicate your first waking hour you will have successfully achieved the following:

- YOU WILL have developed a more intimate relationship with your Heavenly Father, His Son Jesus Christ, and the Holy Spirit.

- YOU WILL have a more clear and better understanding of God's will and purpose for your life.

- YOU WILL have read the entire New Testament by reading for only 20 minutes each day.

- YOU WILL have read all of the book of Proverbs by reading only a Proverb each day.

- YOU WILL have memorized The Ten Commandments.

- YOU WILL have achieved a closer relationship with your wife, your children and your friends.

- YOU WILL have attained a higher self-esteem.

- YOU WILL feel healthier and be more physically fit.

- YOU WILL be on your way to becoming the man God intended you to be.

The Seven Simple Steps

Follow these seven simple steps and you will be successful in completing this course. Stick to it and <u>God will</u> begin to make drastic changes in your life!

1. WAKE UP TIME - God wants you to rise early each day. Set a time and stick to it. This needs to be uninterrupted time. By giving your first waking hour to God in prayer, your entire day will improve. He wants to be involved in even the smallest details throughout your day.

2. MORNING PRAYERS - 30 Minutes – Prayer is the most powerful weapon you have! God <u>promises</u> to answer the prayers of the righteous according to His will. We have included prayers in this book that you can use as a guideline on how to pray for specific areas in your life in addition to your own prayers. Some people find it helpful, especially during the first few days, to read out loud. Reading aloud can be helpful in concentrating and becoming comfortable with the prayer sequence. [*morning prayers begin on page 85*]

3. BIBLE READING – **30 Minutes** - God's Word is alive! It is our rule book and manual for everyday life. By reading just 25 minutes a day, you will have completed the <u>entire</u> New Testament and the complete Book of Proverbs by the end of this course! Save the last five minutes to relax and listen to God.

4. WORKOUT - This is a crucial part of the program. God wants you to take care of your body. If you already have a work out regime, then stick to it. We would encourage you to get a minimum of two hours of exercise a week. You will feel and see the difference in 30 days!

5. RETURN HOME - It is important to be consistent with the time you come home. Your family needs the security of a consistent leader.

6. TIME WITH CHILDREN - 1/2 hr. Minimum, Plus Bedtime Prayer - It is important that you devote quality time each day to your children. The power of the word "Dad" reaches beyond a youngster's childhood. In fact, it spans for generations. Commit to this quality time and you will see a drastic improvement in your children and in your relationship with them.

7. TIME WITH WIFE - 1 hr. Minimum, Plus Bedtime Prayer - Commit to a minimum of one hour of quality time each day with your wife. Pray each night with her. This may be uncomfortable at first, so start out with just a very short prayer. Each night will get easier, and God will take over. Remember a couple that prays together…stays together. You will see an unbelievable improvement in your Marriage and in your relationship with her.

Make a commitment to get up at the same time each morning. Put an X in the Yes box if you were successful or an X in the No box if you were not. Then write in the **actual** time. Continue to do the same process with the remaining six steps.

Proverbs 6:9-13

"How long will you lie there, you sluggard?

When will you get up from your sleep?   A little sleep, a little slumber,

A little folding of the hands to rest, and poverty will come on you

Like a bandit and scarcity like an armed man."

ACTION	YES	NO	ACTUAL
1. Wake up time _____ am			
2. **Morning Prayers - 30 Minutes** *(Page 85)*			
3. **Bible Reading - 30 Minutes**			
A. Proverbs Chapter 1 *(5 minutes)*			
B. Matthew 1-9 *(20 minutes)*			
C. Listening to God *(5 minutes)*			
4. **Workout** *(minimum 15 minutes)*			

ACTION	YES	NO	ACTUAL
5. **Return Home - Goal** _____ am/pm			
6. **Time with Children** *(1/2 hour minimum + bedtime prayer)*			
7. **Time with Wife** *(1 hour minimum + bedtime prayer)*			

The Ten Commandments *(Memorize)*

1. You shall have no other gods before Me.

Daily Devotion

He holds victory in store for the upright,

He is a shield to those whose walk is blameless,

For He guards the course of the just and protects

The way of His faithful ones.

Proverbs 2:7-8

IMPORTANT!

Use this journal space on each day to record significant events as they happen. Expect to see things happen in your life. Record your experiences, events, feelings, and <u>confirmations</u> each day. Jot down your experiences during prayer time, your relationship with your wife, changes in your children, or other differences you notice. Some days you will have nothing to write. Other days you will run out to space.

You may not be used to writing things down. You may not be a natural "journaler" but I encourage you to give it a try. Not only has journaling been shown to help develop self-awareness, but your journal will create a permanent reminder of God's work during your 30 day First Hour journey

Journal _____

Write it down!

Day 2

ACTION	YES	NO	ACTUAL
1. Wake up time _____ am			
2. **Morning Prayers - 30 Minutes** *(Page 85)*			
3. **Bible Reading - 30 Minutes**			
A. Proverbs Chapter 2 *(5 minutes)*			
B. Matthew 10-15 *(20 minutes)*			
C. Listening to God *(5 minutes)*			
4. **Workout** *(minimum 15 minutes)*			

ACTION	YES	NO	ACTUAL
5. **Return Home - Goal _____ am/pm**			
6. **Time with Children** *(1/2 hour minimum + bedtime prayer)*			
7. **Time with Wife** *(1 hour minimum + bedtime prayer)*			

The Ten Commandments *(Memorize)*

1. You shall have no other gods before Me.
2. You shall not make for yourself an idol.

Daily Devotion

My son, do not forget My teaching, but keep

My Commands in your heart, for they will prolong

Your life many years and bring you prosperity.

Let love and faithfulness never leave you.

Bind them around your neck, write them on the tablet

Of your heart, then you will win favor

And a good name in the sight of God and man.

Proverbs 3:1-4

Journal

Write it down!

Day 3

ACTION	YES	NO	ACTUAL
1. Wake up time _____ am			
2. **Morning Prayers - 30 Minutes** *(Page 85)*			
3. **Bible Reading - 30 Minutes**			
A. Proverbs Chapter 3 *(5 minutes)*			
B. Matthew 16-23 *(20 minutes)*			
C. Listening to God *(5 minutes)*			
4. **Workout** *(minimum 15 minutes)*			

ACTION	YES	NO	ACTUAL
5. **Return Home - Goal** _____ am/pm			
6. **Time with Children** *(1/2 hour minimum + bedtime prayer)*			
7. **Time with Wife** *(1 hour minimum + bedtime prayer)*			

The Ten Commandments *(Memorize)*

1. You shall have no other gods before Me.
2. You shall not make for yourself an idol.
3. You shall not take the Lord's name in vain.

Daily Devotion

Put away perversity from your mouth; keep corrupt talk

Far from your lips. Let your eyes look straight ahead,

Fix your gaze directly before you.

Proverbs 4:24-27

Journal

ACTION	YES	NO	ACTUAL
1. **Wake up time** _____ **am**			
2. **Morning Prayers - 30 Minutes** *(Page 85)*			
3. **Bible Reading - 30 Minutes**			
A. Proverbs Chapter 4 *(5 minutes)*			
B. Matthew 24-28 *(20 minutes)*			
C. Listening to God *(5 minutes)*			
4. **Workout** *(minimum 15 minutes)*			

ACTION	YES	NO	ACTUAL
5. **Return Home - Goal** _____ **am/pm**			
6. **Time with Children** *(1/2 hour minimum + bedtime prayer)*			
7. **Time with Wife** *(1 hour minimum + bedtime prayer)*			

The Ten Commandments *(Memorize)*

1. You shall have no other gods before Me.
2. You shall not make for yourself an idol.
3. You shall not take the Lord's name in vain.
4. Remember the Sabbath day by keeping it holy.

Daily Devotion

For a man's ways are in full view of the Lord;

And he examines all his paths. The evil deeds of

A wicked man ensnare him; The cords of his sin

Hold him fast. He will die for lack of discipline

Led astray by his own great folly.

Proverbs 5:21-23

Journal _____

Day 5

ACTION	YES	NO	ACTUAL
1. Wake up time _____ am			
2. **Morning Prayers - 30 Minutes** *(Page 85)*			
3. **Bible Reading - 30 Minutes**			
A. Proverbs Chapter 5 *(5 minutes)*			
B. Mark 1-7 *(20 minutes)*			
C. Listening to God *(5 minutes)*			
4. **Workout** *(minimum 15 minutes)*			

ACTION	YES	NO	ACTUAL
5. **Return Home - Goal** _____ am/pm			
6. **Time with Children** *(1/2 hour minimum + bedtime prayer)*			
7. **Time with Wife** *(1 hour minimum + bedtime prayer)*			

The Ten Commandments *(Memorize)*

1. You shall have no other gods before Me.
2. You shall not make for yourself an idol.
3. You shall not take the Lord's name in vain.
4. Remember the Sabbath day by keeping it holy.
5. Honor your father and your mother.

Daily Devotion

But a man who commits adultery lacks judgment;

Whoever does so destroys himself. Blows and disgrace

Are his lot, and his shame will never be wiped away.

Proverbs 6:32-33

Journal _____

Day 6

ACTION	YES	NO	ACTUAL
1. **Wake up time** _____ am			
2. **Morning Prayers - 30 Minutes** *(Page 85)*			
3. **Bible Reading - 30 Minutes**			
A. Proverbs Chapter 6 *(5 minutes)*			
B. Mark 8-13 *(20 minutes)*			
C. Listening to God *(5 minutes)*			
4. **Workout** *(minimum 15 minutes)*			

ACTION	YES	NO	ACTUAL
5. **Return Home - Goal** _____ am/pm			
6. **Time with Children** *(1/2 hour minimum + bedtime prayer)*			
7. **Time with Wife** *(1 hour minimum + bedtime prayer)*			

The Ten Commandments *(Memorize)*

1. You shall have no other gods before Me.
2. You shall not make for yourself an idol.
3. You shall not take the Lord's name in vain.
4. Remember the Sabbath day by keeping it holy.
5. Honor your father and your mother.
6. You shall not murder.

Daily Devotion

My son, keep My words

And store up My commands within you.

Keep My commands and you will live;

Guard My teachings as the apple of your eye.

Proverbs 7:1-3

Journal

Day 7

ACTION	YES	NO	ACTUAL
1. Wake up time _____ am			
2. Morning Prayers - 30 Minutes *(Page 85)*			
3. Bible Reading - 30 Minutes			
A. Proverbs Chapter 7 *(5 minutes)*			
B. Mark 14-16, Luke 1-3 *(20 minutes)*			
C. Listening to God *(5 minutes)*			
4. Workout *(minimum 15 minutes)*			

ACTION	YES	NO	ACTUAL
5. Return Home - Goal _____ am/pm			
6. Time with Children *(1/2 hour minimum + bedtime prayer)*			
7. Time with Wife *(1 hour minimum + bedtime prayer)*			

The Ten Commandments *(Memorize)*

1. You shall have no other gods before Me.
2. You shall not make for yourself an idol.
3. You shall not take the Lord's name in vain.
4. Remember the Sabbath day by keeping it holy.
5. Honor your father and your mother.
6. You shall not murder.
7. You shall not commit adultery.

Daily Devotion

Now then, My sons, listen to Me.

Blessed are those who keep My ways.

Listen to My instruction and be wise. Do not ignore it.

Blessed is the man who listens to Me, watching daily

At My doors, waiting at My doorway. For whoever finds Me,

Finds life and receives favor from the Lord.

Proverbs 8:32-35

Journal

Day 8

ACTION	YES	NO	ACTUAL
1. Wake up time _____ am			
2. Morning Prayers - 30 Minutes *(Page 85)*			
3. Bible Reading - 30 Minutes			
A. Proverbs Chapter 8 *(5 minutes)*			
B. Luke 4-8 *(20 minutes)*			
C. Listening to God *(5 minutes)*			
4. Workout *(minimum 15 minutes)*			

ACTION	YES	NO	ACTUAL
5. Return Home - Goal _____ am/pm			
6. Time with Children *(1/2 hour minimum + bedtime prayer)*			
7. Time with Wife *(1 hour minimum + bedtime prayer)*			

The Ten Commandments *(Memorize)*

1. You shall have no other gods before Me.
2. You shall not make for yourself an idol.
3. You shall not take the Lord's name in vain.
4. Remember the Sabbath day by keeping it holy.
5. Honor your father and your mother.
6. You shall not murder.
7. You shall not commit adultery.
8. You shall not steal.

Daily Devotion

The fear of the Lord is the beginning of wisdom,

And knowledge of the Holy One is understanding,

For through Me, your days will be many,

And years will be added to your life.

Proverbs 9:10-12

Journal _____

Day 9

ACTION	YES	NO	ACTUAL
1. Wake up time _____ am			
2. **Morning Prayers - 30 Minutes** *(Page 85)*			
3. **Bible Reading - 30 Minutes**			
A. Proverbs Chapter 9 *(5 minutes)*			
B. Luke 9-14 *(20 minutes)*			
C. Listening to God *(5 minutes)*			
4. **Workout** *(minimum 15 minutes)*			

ACTION	YES	NO	ACTUAL
5. **Return Home - Goal** _____ am/pm			
6. **Time with Children** *(1/2 hour minimum + bedtime prayer)*			
7. **Time with Wife** *(1 hour minimum + bedtime prayer)*			

The Ten Commandments *(Memorize)*

1. You shall have no other gods before Me.
2. You shall not make for yourself an idol.
3. You shall not take the Lord's name in vain.
4. Remember the Sabbath day by keeping it holy.
5. Honor your father and your mother.
6. You shall not murder.
7. You shall not commit adultery.
8. You shall not steal.
9. You shall not give false testimony against your neighbor.

Daily Devotion

Ill-gotten treasures are of no value,

But righteousness delivers from death.

The Lord does not let the righteous go hungry,

But He thwarts the craving of the wicked.

Proverbs 10:2-4

Journal

Day 10

ACTION	YES	NO	ACTUAL
1. Wake up time _____ am			
2. **Morning Prayers - 30 Minutes** *(Page 85)*			
3. **Bible Reading - 30 Minutes**			
A. Proverbs Chapter 10 *(5 minutes)*			
B. Luke 15-21 *(20 minutes)*			
C. Listening to God *(5 minutes)*			
4. **Workout** *(minimum 15 minutes)*			

ACTION	YES	NO	ACTUAL
5. **Return Home - Goal _____ am/pm**			
6. **Time with Children** *(1/2 hour minimum + bedtime prayer)*			
7. **Time with Wife** *(1 hour minimum + bedtime prayer)*			

The Ten Commandments *(Memorize)*

1. You shall have no other gods before Me.
2. You shall not make for yourself an idol.
3. You shall not take the Lord's name in vain.
4. Remember the Sabbath day by keeping it holy.
5. Honor your father and your mother.
6. You shall not murder.
7. You shall not commit adultery.
8. You shall not steal.
9. You shall not give false testimony against your neighbor.
10. You shall not covet your neighbor's wife.

Daily Devotion

One man gives freely, yet gains even more;

Another withholds unduly, but comes to poverty.

A generous man will prosper; he who refreshes

Others will himself be refreshed.

Proverbs 11:24-25

Journal

Day 11

ACTION	YES	NO	ACTUAL
1. Wake up time _____ am			
2. Morning Prayers - 30 Minutes *(Page 85)*			
3. Bible Reading - 30 Minutes			
A. Proverbs Chapter 11 *(5 minutes)*			
B. Luke 22-24, John 1-3 *(20 minutes)*			
C. Listening to God *(5 minutes)*			
4. Workout *(minimum 15 minutes)*			

ACTION	YES	NO	ACTUAL
5. Return Home - Goal _____ am/pm			
6. Time with Children *(1/2 hour minimum + bedtime prayer)*			
7. Time with Wife *(1 hour minimum + bedtime prayer)*			

The Ten Commandments *(Write them)*

1. _____

Daily Devotion

No harm befalls the righteous, but the wicked have

Their fill of trouble. The Lord detests lying lips,

But He delights in men who are truthful.

Proverbs 12:21-22

Journal

Day 12

ACTION	YES	NO	ACTUAL
1. Wake up time _____ am			
2. **Morning Prayers - 30 Minutes** *(Page 85)*			
3. **Bible Reading - 30 Minutes**			
A. Proverbs Chapter 12 *(5 minutes)*			
B. John 4-8 *(20 minutes)*			
C. Listening to God *(5 minutes)*			
4. **Workout** *(minimum 15 minutes)*			

ACTION	YES	NO	ACTUAL
5. **Return Home - Goal** _____ am/pm			
6. **Time with Children** *(1/2 hour minimum + bedtime prayer)*			
7. **Time with Wife** *(1 hour minimum + bedtime prayer)*			

The Ten Commandments *(Write them)*

1. _____

2. _____

Daily Devotion

Misfortune pursues the sinner,

But prosperity is the reward of the righteous.

A good man leaves an inheritance

For his children's children,

But a sinner's wealth is stored up for the righteous.

Proverbs 13:21-22

Journal

ACTION	YES	NO	ACTUAL
1. Wake up time _____ am			
2. **Morning Prayers - 30 Minutes** *(Page 85)*			
3. **Bible Reading - 30 Minutes**			
A. Proverbs Chapter 13 *(5 minutes)*			
B. John 9-16 *(20 minutes)*			
C. Listening to God *(5 minutes)*			
4. **Workout** *(minimum 15 minutes)*			

ACTION	YES	NO	ACTUAL
5. **Return Home - Goal** _____ am/pm			
6. **Time with Children** *(1/2 hour minimum + bedtime prayer)*			
7. **Time with Wife** *(1 hour minimum + bedtime prayer)*			

The Ten Commandments *(Write them)*

1. _____

2. _____

3. _____

Daily Devotion

He who fears the Lord has a secure fortress,

And for his children, it will be refuge.

The fear of the Lord is a fountain of life,

Turning a man from the snares of death.

Proverbs 14:26-27

Journal

Day 14

ACTION	YES	NO	ACTUAL
1. Wake up time _____ am			
2. Morning Prayers - 30 Minutes *(Page 85)*			
3. Bible Reading - 30 Minutes			
A. Proverbs Chapter 14 *(5 minutes)*			
B. John 17-21, Acts 1-2 *(20 minutes)*			
C. Listening to God *(5 minutes)*			
4. Workout *(minimum 15 minutes)*			

ACTION	YES	NO	ACTUAL
5. Return Home - Goal _____ am/pm			
6. Time with Children *(1/2 hour minimum + bedtime prayer)*			
7. Time with Wife *(1 hour minimum + bedtime prayer)*			

The Ten Commandments *(Write them)*

1. _____
2. _____
3. _____
4. _____

Daily Devotion

The Lord detests the sacrifice of the wicked,

But the prayer of the upright pleases Him.

The Lord detests the way of the wicked,

But He loves those who pursue righteousness.

Stern discipline awaits him who leaves the path;

He who hates correction will die.

Proverbs 15:8-10

Journal

Day 15

ACTION	YES	NO	ACTUAL
1. **Wake up time** _____ am			
2. **Morning Prayers - 30 Minutes** *(Page 85)*			
3. **Bible Reading - 30 Minutes**			
A. Proverbs Chapter 15 *(5 minutes)*			
B. Acts 3-9 *(20 minutes)*			
C. Listening to God *(5 minutes)*			
4. **Workout** *(minimum 15 minutes)*			

ACTION	YES	NO	ACTUAL
5. **Return Home - Goal** _____ am/pm			
6. **Time with Children** *(1/2 hour minimum + bedtime prayer)*			
7. **Time with Wife** *(1 hour minimum + bedtime prayer)*			

The Ten Commandments *(Write them)*

1. _____
2. _____
3. _____
4. _____
5. _____

Daily Devotion

Commit to the Lord whatever you do,

And your plans will succeed. The Lord works out

Everything for His own ends.

Proverbs 16:3-4

Journal

Day 16

ACTION	YES	NO	ACTUAL
1. **Wake up time** _____ **am**			
2. **Morning Prayers - 30 Minutes** *(Page 85)*			
3. **Bible Reading - 30 Minutes**			
A. Proverbs Chapter 16 *(5 minutes)*			
B. Acts 10-17 *(20 minutes)*			
C. Listening to God *(5 minutes)*			
4. **Workout** *(minimum 15 minutes)*			

ACTION	YES	NO	ACTUAL
5. **Return Home - Goal** _____ **am/pm**			
6. **Time with Children** *(1/2 hour minimum + bedtime prayer)*			
7. **Time with Wife** *(1 hour minimum + bedtime prayer)*			

The Ten Commandments *(Write them)*

1. _____
2. _____
3. _____
4. _____
5. _____
6. _____

Daily Devotion

A man of knowledge uses words with restraint, and a

Man of understanding is even-tempered.

Proverbs 17:27

Journal

ACTION	YES	NO	ACTUAL
1. **Wake up time** _____ am			
2. **Morning Prayers - 30 Minutes** *(Page 85)*			
3. **Bible Reading - 30 Minutes**			
A. Proverbs Chapter 17 *(5 minutes)*			
B. Acts 18-25 *(20 minutes)*			
C. Listening to God *(5 minutes)*			
4. **Workout** *(minimum 15 minutes)*			

ACTION	YES	NO	ACTUAL
5. **Return Home - Goal** _____ am/pm			
6. **Time with Children** *(1/2 hour minimum + bedtime prayer)*			
7. **Time with Wife** *(1 hour minimum + bedtime prayer)*			

The Ten Commandments *(Write them)*

1. _____
2. _____
3. _____
4. _____
5. _____
6. _____
7. _____

Daily Devotion

The name of the Lord is a strong tower;

The righteous run to it and are safe.

The heart of the discerning acquires knowledge;

The ears of the wise seek it out.

Proverbs 18:10-15

Journal

Day 18

ACTION	YES	NO	ACTUAL
1. Wake up time _____ am			
2. **Morning Prayers - 30 Minutes** *(Page 85)*			
3. **Bible Reading - 30 Minutes**			
A. Proverbs Chapter 18 *(5 minutes)*			
B. Acts 26-28, Romans 1-5 *(20 minutes)*			
C. Listening to God *(5 minutes)*			
4. **Workout** *(minimum 15 minutes)*			

ACTION	YES	NO	ACTUAL
5. **Return Home - Goal _____ am/pm**			
6. **Time with Children** *(1/2 hour minimum + bedtime prayer)*			
7. **Time with Wife** *(1 hour minimum + bedtime prayer)*			

The Ten Commandments *(Write them)*

1. _____
2. _____
3. _____
4. _____
5. _____
6. _____
7. _____
8. _____

Daily Devotion

Listen to advice and accept instruction,

And in the end you will be wise.

Many are the plans in a man's heart;

But it is the Lord's purpose that prevails.

Stop listening to instruction, My son,

And you will stray from the words of knowledge.

Proverbs 19:20-21, 27

Journal

ACTION	YES	NO	ACTUAL
1. Wake up time _____ am			
2. Morning Prayers - 30 Minutes *(Page 85)*			
3. Bible Reading - 30 Minutes			
A. Proverbs Chapter 19 *(5 minutes)*			
B. Romans 6-16 *(20 minutes)*			
C. Listening to God *(5 minutes)*			
4. Workout *(minimum 15 minutes)*			

ACTION	YES	NO	ACTUAL
5. Return Home - Goal _____ am/pm			
6. Time with Children *(1/2 hour minimum + bedtime prayer)*			
7. Time with Wife *(1 hour minimum + bedtime prayer)*			

The Ten Commandments *(Write them)*

1. _____
2. _____
3. _____
4. _____
5. _____
6. _____
7. _____
8. _____
9. _____

Daily Devotion

Do not love sleep, or you will grow poor;

Stay awake and you will have food to spare.

Proverbs 20:13-24

Journal

Day 20

ACTION	YES	NO	ACTUAL
1. Wake up time _____ am			
2. **Morning Prayers - 30 Minutes** *(Page 85)*			
3. **Bible Reading - 30 Minutes**			
A. Proverbs Chapter 20 *(5 minutes)*			
B. 1 Corinthians 1-11 *(20 minutes)*			
C. Listening to God *(5 minutes)*			
4. **Workout** *(minimum 15 minutes)*			

ACTION	YES	NO	ACTUAL
5. **Return Home - Goal _____ am/pm**			
6. **Time with Children** *(1/2 hour minimum + bedtime prayer)*			
7. **Time with Wife** *(1 hour minimum + bedtime prayer)*			

The Ten Commandments *(Write them)*

1. _____
2. _____
3. _____
4. _____
5. _____
6. _____
7. _____
8. _____
9. _____
10. _____

Daily Devotion

He who pursues righteousness and love

Finds life, prosperity and honor.

Proverbs 21:21

Journal

Day 21

ACTION	YES	NO	ACTUAL
1. Wake up time _____ am			
2. Morning Prayers - 30 Minutes *(Page 85)*			
3. Bible Reading - 30 Minutes			
A. Proverbs Chapter 21 *(5 minutes)*			
B. 1 Corinthians 12-16, 2 Corinthians 1-6 *(20 minutes)*			
C. Listening to God *(5 minutes)*			
4. Workout *(minimum 15 minutes)*			

ACTION	YES	NO	ACTUAL
5. Return Home - Goal _____ am/pm			
6. Time with Children *(1/2 hour minimum + bedtime prayer)*			
7. Time with Wife *(1 hour minimum + bedtime prayer)*			

Again, I tell you that if two of you on earth agree
About anything you ask for, it will be done for you by
My Father in heaven. For where two or three come
Together in My name, there am I with them.
Matthew 18:19-20

Daily Devotion

Train a child in the way he should go,

And when he is old he will not turn from it.

Proverbs 22:6

Journal

ACTION	YES	NO	ACTUAL
1. Wake up time _____ am			
2. Morning Prayers - 30 Minutes *(Page 85)*			
3. Bible Reading - 30 Minutes			
A. Proverbs Chapter 22 *(5 minutes)*			
B. 2 Corinthians 7-13, Galatians 1-3 *(20 minutes)*			
C. Listening to God *(5 minutes)*			
4. Workout *(minimum 15 minutes)*			

ACTION	YES	NO	ACTUAL
5. Return Home - Goal _____ am/pm			
6. Time with Children *(1/2 hour minimum + bedtime prayer)*			
7. Time with Wife *(1 hour minimum + bedtime prayer)*			

The Lord detests the sacrifice of the wicked,

But the prayer of the upright pleases him.

The Lord detests the way of the wicked but

He loves those who Pursue righteousness.

Proverbs 15:8-9

Daily Devotion

Do not wear yourself out to get rich;

Have the wisdom to show restraint.

Cast but a glance at riches, and they are gone,

For they will surely sprout wings and fly off

To the sky like an eagle.

Proverbs 23:4-5

Journal

ACTION	YES	NO	ACTUAL
1. Wake up time _____ am			
2. **Morning Prayers - 30 Minutes** *(Page 85)*			
3. **Bible Reading - 30 Minutes**			
A. Proverbs Chapter 23 *(5 minutes)*			
B. Galatians 4-6, Ephesians 1-6 *(20 minutes)*			
C. Listening to God *(5 minutes)*			
4. **Workout** *(minimum 15 minutes)*			

ACTION	YES	NO	ACTUAL
5. **Return Home - Goal** _____ am/pm			
6. **Time with Children** *(1/2 hour minimum + bedtime prayer)*			
7. **Time with Wife** *(1 hour minimum + bedtime prayer)*			

Therefore, I tell you, whatever you ask for in prayer,
Believe that you have received it, and it will be yours.
And when you stand praying, if you hold anything
Against anyone, forgive him, so that your Father in
Heaven may forgive you your sins.

Mark 11:24-26

Daily Devotion

By wisdom a house is built and through understanding

It is established; through knowledge its rooms

Are filled with rare and beautiful treasures.

Proverbs 24:3-4

Journal

Day 24

ACTION	YES	NO	ACTUAL
1. **Wake up time** _____ **am**			
2. **Morning Prayers - 30 Minutes** *(Page 85)*			
3. **Bible Reading - 30 Minutes**			
A. Proverbs Chapter 24 *(5 minutes)*			
B. Phil 1-4, Col 1-4, 1 Thes 1-5 *(20 minutes)*			
C. Listening to God *(5 minutes)*			
4. **Workout** *(minimum 15 minutes)*			

ACTION	YES	NO	ACTUAL
5. **Return Home - Goal** _____ **am/pm**			
6. **Time with Children** *(1/2 hour minimum + bedtime prayer)*			
7. **Time with Wife** *(1 hour minimum + bedtime prayer)*			

Do not be anxious about anything, but in everything,

By prayer and petition, with thanksgiving,

Present your requests to God. And the peace of God,

Which transcends all understanding, will guard your

Hearts and your minds in Christ Jesus.

Philippians 4:6-7

Daily Devotion

Like a city whose walls are broken down,

Is a man who lacks self-control.

Proverbs 25:28

Journal

ACTION	YES	NO	ACTUAL
1. Wake up time _____ am			
2. **Morning Prayers - 30 Minutes** *(Page 85)*			
3. **Bible Reading - 30 Minutes**			
A. Proverbs Chapter 25 *(5 minutes)*			
B. 2 Thes 1-3, 1 Tim 1-6, 2 Tim 1-4 *(20 minutes)*			
C. Listening to God *(5 minutes)*			
4. **Workout** *(minimum 15 minutes)*			

ACTION	YES	NO	ACTUAL
5. **Return Home - Goal** _____ am/pm			
6. **Time with Children** *(1/2 hour minimum + bedtime prayer)*			
7. **Time with Wife** *(1 hour minimum + bedtime prayer)*			

And the prayer offered in faith will make the sick well;
The Lord will raise him up. If he has sinned, he will be
Forgiven. Therefore confess your sins to each other and
Pray for each other so that you may be healed. The
Prayer of a righteous man is powerful and effective.
James 5:15-16

Daily Devotion

The words of a gossip are like choice morsels;

They go down to a man's inmost parts.

Proverbs 26:22

Journal

Day 26

ACTION	YES	NO	ACTUAL
1. Wake up time _____ am			
2. **Morning Prayers - 30 Minutes** *(Page 85)*			
3. **Bible Reading - 30 Minutes**			
A. Proverbs Chapter 26 *(5 minutes)*			
B. Titus 1-3, Philemon, Hebrews 1-9 *(20 minutes)*			
C. Listening to God *(5 minutes)*			
4. **Workout** *(minimum 15 minutes)*			

ACTION	YES	NO	ACTUAL
5. **Return Home - Goal _____ am/pm**			
6. **Time with Children** *(1/2 hour minimum + bedtime prayer)*			
7. **Time with Wife** *(1 hour minimum + bedtime prayer)*			

For the eyes of the Lord are on the righteous

And his ears are attentive to their prayer,

But the face of the Lord is against those who do evil.

1 Peter 3:12

Daily Devotion

Be sure you know the condition of your flocks,

Give careful attention to your herds;

For riches do not endure forever,

And a crown is not secure for all generations.

Proverbs 27:23-24

Journal

Day 27

ACTION	YES	NO	ACTUAL
1. Wake up time _____ am			
2. **Morning Prayers - 30 Minutes** *(Page 85)*			
3. **Bible Reading - 30 Minutes**			
A. Proverbs Chapter 27 *(5 minutes)*			
B. Hebrews 10-13, James 1-5 *(20 minutes)*			
C. Listening to God *(5 minutes)*			
4. **Workout** *(minimum 15 minutes)*			

ACTION	YES	NO	ACTUAL
5. **Return Home - Goal** _____ am/pm			
6. **Time with Children** *(1/2 hour minimum + bedtime prayer)*			
7. **Time with Wife** *(1 hour minimum + bedtime prayer)*			

They were helped in fighting them, and God handed the Hagrites and all their allies over to them because they Cried out to Him during the battle. He answered their Prayers, because they trusted in Him.

1 Chronicles 5:20

Daily Devotion

He who gives to the poor will lack nothing,

But he who closes his eyes to them receives many curses.

Proverbs 28:27

Journal

ACTION	YES	NO	ACTUAL
1. **Wake up time** _____ **am**			
2. **Morning Prayers - 30 Minutes** *(Page 85)*			
3. **Bible Reading - 30 Minutes**			
A. Proverbs Chapter 28 *(5 minutes)*			
B. 1 Peter 1-5, 2 Peter 1-3, 1 John 1-4 *(20 minutes)*			
C. Listening to God *(5 minutes)*			
4. **Workout** *(minimum 15 minutes)*			

ACTION	YES	NO	ACTUAL
5. **Return Home - Goal** _____ **am/pm**			
6. **Time with Children** *(1/2 hour minimum + bedtime prayer)*			
7. **Time with Wife** *(1 hour minimum + bedtime prayer)*			

What other nation is so great as to have their gods

Near them the way the Lord our God is near us

Whenever we pray to Him?

Deuteronomy 4:7-8

Daily Devotion

A fool gives full vent to his anger,

But a wise man keeps himself under control.

Proverbs 29:11

Journal

Day 29

ACTION	YES	NO	ACTUAL
1. Wake up time _____ am			
2. **Morning Prayers - 30 Minutes** *(Page 85)*			
3. **Bible Reading - 30 Minutes**			
A. Proverbs Chapter 29 *(5 minutes)*			
B. 2 John, 3 John, Jude, Revelation 1-6 *(20 minutes)*			
C. Listening to God *(5 minutes)*			
4. **Workout** *(minimum 15 minutes)*			

ACTION	YES	NO	ACTUAL
5. **Return Home - Goal** _____ am/pm			
6. **Time with Children** *(1/2 hour minimum + bedtime prayer)*			
7. **Time with Wife** *(1 hour minimum + bedtime prayer)*			

But I tell you: Love your enemies

And pray for those who persecute you,

That you may be sons of your Father in heaven.

Matthew 5:44

Day 30

ACTION	YES	NO	ACTUAL
1. Wake up time _____ am			
2. Morning Prayers - 30 Minutes *(Page 85)*			
3. Bible Reading - 30 Minutes			
A. Proverbs Chapter 30 *(5 minutes)*			
B. Revelation 7-22 *(20 minutes)*			
C. Listening to God *(5 minutes)*			
4. Workout *(minimum 15 minutes)*			

ACTION	YES	NO	ACTUAL
5. Return Home - Goal _____ am/pm			
6. Time with Children *(1/2 hour minimum + bedtime prayer)*			
7. Time with Wife *(1 hour minimum + bedtime prayer)*			

Speak up for those who cannot speak for themselves,

For the rights of all who are destitute. Speak up and

Judge fairly; defend the rights of the poor and needy.

Proverbs 31:8

Congratulations!

The past 30 days have been a great start to beginning a daily discipline of spending time with God and your family. As you continue your spiritual journey, there are two great callings that God has for you in life. They are explained in the Bible verses below:

The Great Commandment

"You must love the Lord your God with all your heart,
all your soul, all your mind, and all your strength. The second
is equally important: 'Love your neighbor as yourself.'
No other commandment is greater than these."
Matthew 22:37-40

The Great Commission

"Then Jesus came to them and said, "All authority in heaven
and on earth has been given to Me. Therefore, go and make disciples of all
nations, baptizing them in the name of the Father and of the Son and of the
Holy Spirit, and teaching them to obey
everything I have commanded you, and surely
I am with you always, to the very end of the age."
Matthew 28:18-20

In order to help you strengthen and build on the commitments you have made these past 30 days, take a few moments to read the next two pages and make a covenant and a commitment to continue to live out God's plan for your life by giving Him the first part of your day.

The Great Commandment Covenant

Loving God

Today, I make a covenant with God to continue to give Him the first part of my day. I realize that without spending time with Him on a daily basis, I will not be prepared to face the challenges that life brings. I will faithfully continue to read God's Word, pray, and serve Him with everything I have. My goal will be to love God with my whole heart and life. I will also love and serve God by treating my body as His temple.

Loving Others

Today, I make a covenant with God to love others as I love myself. This will begin with my wife (if married). I will treat her with the love and respect she deserves and strive to be the servant leader God has called me to be in my home. I will also focus on giving my children (if you have children) the love and time that they need so that they will see the example of Christ in me. Finally, I will make a conscious choice to allow Christ's love to flow through me as I come into contact with others on a daily basis.

I _____ , enter into this covenant

on this_____ day of_____ ,_____ .

_____

Signature

The Great Commission Commitment

You have been drafted by God to join His army and to rise up for this great nation. Your commitment to this program will not only change your life and the lives of your family, but the lives of thousands of other families through your commitment to give this book to five other men, who will in turn share it with five other men, and the cycle will go on and on and continue to grow rapidly. We all know the power of duplication in MLM companies. This is MLM…Multi-Level Ministry!!

At the beginning of this book you made three commitments, 1) To following the study guide for the next 30 days, 2) To follow all 7 simple steps of *The First Hour* program, 3) To do your part in the Great Commission by sharing this book with five other men. Write down the names of TWO of your Christian brothers that you feel would benefit from this book. These can be men from your Church, your work, or anyone that you know that already has a personal relationship with Jesus Christ.

1. _____   2. _____

Next, write down the names of THREE men that you feel do not have a personal relationship with Jesus Christ. Pray for God to put these men on your heart! Listen to the Lord and then go and speak to them. Hand them this book and let the Holy Spirit do the rest!

1. _____   2. _____

3. _____

Please visit www.thefirsthour.com for additional copies of *The First Hour for Men*, other books in the *First Hour* devotional series, and related materials and information to support the *First Hour* mission. Thank you for your prayers and commitment to partner with us as we spread the message of Jesus Christ and encourage others to dedicate their *First Hour* to God each day!

To Accept Jesus Christ
Into My Life

Prayer of Salvation

Lord Jesus,

I confess that I am a sinner, and I ask that You forgive me. I do believe that You died on the cross for my sins, and rose again from the dead to give me eternal life. Lord, today I confess You are God, I ask You to come into my heart, and I accept You as my personal Savior. Forgive me of all of my sins, wash me clean, and give me a fresh start. From this day forward take control of my life, and make me the man that You designed me to be. In Your most precious name I pray, Amen.

Morning Prayers
(30 Minutes Daily)

The Power of Prayer

The prayers in this book are your essential primer for learning how to pray effectively. When you pray according to the Scriptures, you can be assured that you are praying in line with God's will and that He will honor His word. Let these powerful prayers help you discover His best for you, your family, and your career.

Deliberately pray and meditate on each prayer. Allow the Holy Spirit to make the Word a reality in your heart. Your spirit will become alive to God's Word. You will find yourself pouring over His word, hungering for more and more. Remember, the Father promises to reward those who diligently seek Him and promises to answer the prayers of the righteous.

Germaine Copeland
Prayers That Avail Much ®

IMPORTANT

There are 18 prayers in this book. Every prayer has its order and special purpose in preparing you for your day. Please <u>do not skip</u> any of the prayers unless they do not pertain to you, (e.g., wife, husband, children, business owner, etc.), and <u>do not switch the order</u> of them. Pray <u>all</u> the prayers <u>every day</u>. After a few mornings, you should be able to complete them in 30 minutes or less. Also, make sure to read the Scripture on the left page every day.

CONTENTS

We're depending on God; He's everything we need.

What's more, our hearts brim with joy

Since we've taken for our own His Holy Name.

Love us God, with all You've got…

That's what we're depending on.

God First

God is strong, and He wants you strong.
So take everything the Master has set out for you,
Well-made weapons of the best materials,
And put them to use so you will be able to stand up
To everything the devil throws your way.
Ephesians 6:10-11

To Put on the Armor of God

Heavenly Father, I put on the Armor of God with gratitude and praise. You have provided all I need to stand in victory against Satan and his kingdom.

I confidently take the Belt of Truth. Thank You that Satan cannot stand against the bold use of Truth.

Thank You for the Breastplate of Righteousness. I embrace that righteousness which is mine by faith in Jesus Christ. I know that Satan must retreat before the righteousness of God.

You have provided the solid Rock of Peace. I claim the peace with God that is mine through justification. I desire the peace of God that touches my emotions and feelings through prayer and sanctification.

Eagerly, Lord, I lift up the Shield of Faith against all the blazing missiles that Satan fires at me. I know that You are my Shield.

I recognize that my mind is a particular target of Satan's deceiving ways; I cover my mind with the powerful Helmet of Salvation.

With joy, I lift the Sword of the Spirit, which is the Word of God. I choose to live in its Truth and power. Enable me to use Your Word to defend myself from Satan, and also to wield the Sword well, to push Satan back, to defeat him.

Thank You, dear Lord, for prayer. Help me to keep this Armor well oiled with prayer. All these petitions I offer You through the mighty name of our Lord Jesus Christ. Amen.

Scripture References

Ephesians 6:11-14	Psalm 34:14
2 Corinthians 10:4	Ephesians 6:16, 17
Ephesians 6:14, 15	1 John 4:4

Because of the sacrifice of the Messiah,
His blood poured out on the altar of the Cross.
We're a free people—free of penalties and
Punishments, chalked up by all our misdeeds,
And not just barely free either; abundantly free!
Ephesians 1:7

To Receive and Walk in Forgiveness

Father, Your Word declares that if I ask for forgiveness, You will forgive and cleanse me from all unrighteousness. Help me to receive forgiveness for my sins. Help me to forgive myself, Father. Your Son, Jesus, said that whatever I ask for in prayer, having faith, and really believing I will receive it according to Your will.

In the face of this feeling of guilt and unworthiness, I receive my forgiveness, and the pressure is gone—my guilt dissolved, my sin disappeared. I am blessed, for You have forgiven my transgressions—You have covered my sins. I get a fresh start, my slate's clean, for You will never count my sins against me or hold anything back from me.

Father, I repent of holding on to bad feelings toward others. I bind myself to Godly repentance and loose myself from bitterness, resentment, envying, strife, and unkindness in any form. I ask Your forgiveness for the sin of _____. By faith, I receive it, having assurance that I am cleansed from all unrighteousness through the body and blood of Jesus Christ. I forgive all who have wronged and hurt me, and ask You to forgive and release them.

I confess Jesus as my Lord and Savior. He has given me the right to become Your child. I acknowledge You, Lord as my Father. Thank You for forgiving me and absolving me of all guilt. I am an overcomer by the blood of the Lamb and by the word of my testimony.

I resist the temptation to be anxious about anything, but in every circumstance and in everything by prayer and petition with thanksgiving continue to make my wants and the wants of others known to God. Whatever I ask for in prayer, I believe it shall be done for me according to His will. In the name of Jesus, Amen.

Scripture References

John 14:16, 17	Acts 19:2, 5, 6
Luke 11:13	Romans 10:9, 10

But you will receive power when the Holy Spirit

Comes on you; and you will be My witnesses

In Jerusalem, and in all Judea and Samaria,

And to the ends of the earth.

Acts 1:8

To Receive the Infilling of the Holy Spirit

My Heavenly Father, I am Your child, for I believe in my heart that Jesus has been raised from the dead, and I have confessed Him as my Lord and Savior.

Jesus said, "How much more shall your Heavenly Father give the Holy Spirit to those who ask Him." I ask You now in the name of Jesus to fill me with the Holy Spirit. I step into the fullness and power that I desire in the name of Jesus. I confess that I am a Spirit-filled Christian. Whatever I ask for in prayer, I believe that it is granted to me, and I will receive it according to your will. In the name of Jesus. Amen.

Scripture References

Acts 2:4	Acts 19:2, 5, 6
Acts 1:8	Luke 11:13
John 14:16, 17	1 Corinthians 14:2-15:1
1 Corinthians 14:18, 27	

Don't grieve God. Don't break His heart.

His Holy Spirit, moving and breathing in you,

Is the most intimate part of your life,

Making you fit for Himself.

Don't take such a gift for granted.

Ephesians 4:30

To Walk in Sanctification

Father, thank You for sanctifying me by the Truth; Your Word is Truth. Jesus, You consecrated Yourself for my sake, so I will be Truth-consecrated in my mission. In the name of Jesus, I repent and turn from my wicked ways. I wash myself and make myself clean. I cease to do evil, and I am learning to do right.

Father, You dwell in me and walk with me. So I leave the corruption and compromise; I leave it for good. You are my Father, and I will not link up with those who would pollute me, because You want me all for Yourself. I purify myself from everything that contaminates body and spirit, perfecting holiness out of reverence for God.

I submit myself to You, Lord—spirit, soul, and body. I strip myself of my old, unrenewed self and put on the new nature, changing whatever needs to be changed in my life. The desire of my heart is to be a vessel unto honor, sanctified, fitting for the Master's use, and prepared for every good work.

Thank You, Lord, that I eat the good of the land, because You have given me a willing and obedient heart. In the name of Jesus. Amen.

Scripture References

John 17:17, 19	Isaiah 1:16, 17
Ephesians 4:22-24	2 Timothy 2:21
2 Corinthians 6:17	2 Corinthians 7:1

Open up before God, keep nothing back;
He'll do whatever needs to be done: He'll validate
Your life in the clear light of day, and stamp you with
Approval at high noon. Quiet down before God…
Be prayerful before Him.
Psalm 37:5-7

To Pray

Father, in the name of Jesus, I thank You for calling me to be a joint promoter and a laborer together—with You. I commit to pray and not to give up.

Jesus, You are the Son of God, and I will never stop trusting You. You are my High Priest, and You understand my weaknesses. So I come boldly to the throne of my gracious God. There I receive mercy and find grace to help when I need it.

There are times I do not know what to pray for. Holy Spirit, I submit to Your leadership and thank You for interceding for us with groans that words cannot express. You search hearts and know the mind of the spirit, because You intercede for the saints in accordance with God's will.

You made Christ, Who never sinned, to be the offering for our sin, so that we could be made right with You through Christ. Now my earnest, heartfelt, continued prayer makes tremendous power available—dynamic in its working. Father, I live in You—abide vitally united to You—and Your words remain in me and continue to live in my heart. When I produce much fruit, it brings great glory to my Father—the Father of my Lord Jesus Christ. Amen. *(Add your personal daily prayer requests)*

Scripture References

1 Corinthians 3:9	Mark 11:24
Luke 18:1 NIV	2 Corinthians 5:21
Romans 8:26, 27	James 5:16
Romans 8:28	John 15:7, 8

DAILY PRAYERS

I'll run the course You lay out for me
If You'll just show me how. God, teach me
Lessons for living so I can stay the course.
Give me insight so I can do what
You tell me my whole life…
One long, obedient response.
Psalm 119:32-34

To Walk in God's Wisdom and His Perfect Will

Father, I ask You to give me a complete understanding of what You want to do in my life, and I ask You to make me wise with spiritual wisdom. Then, the way I live will always honor and please You, and I will continually do good, kind things for others. All the while, I will learn to know You better and better.

I roll my works upon You, Lord, and You make my thoughts agreeable to Your will, so my plans are established and will succeed. You direct my steps and make them sure. I understand and firmly grasp what the will of the Lord is for I am not vague, thoughtless, or foolish. I stand firm and mature in spiritual growth, convinced and fully assured in everything willed by God.

Father, You have destined and appointed me to come progressively to know Your will—that is to perceive, to recognize more strongly and clearly, and to become better and more intimately acquainted with Your will. I thank You, Father, for the Holy Spirit Who abides permanently in me and Who guides me into all the Truth—the whole, full Truth—and speaks whatever He hears from the Father and announces and declares to me the things that are to come. I have the mind of Christ and hold the thoughts, feelings, and purposes of His heart.

So, Father, I have entered into that blessed rest by adhering to, trusting in, and relying on You, as I acknowledge You in all of my ways, You are directing my paths. I believe that as I trust in You completely, You will show me the path of life, in the name of Jesus, Amen.

Scripture References

Revelation 4:11　　　　Acts 22:14
Ephesians 1:5　　　　Hebrews 4:10
Proverbs 16:3, 9　　　Colossians 4:12

My son, if you accept My words and store up
My commands within you, turning your ear to wisdom
And applying your heart to understanding, and if you
Call out for insight and cry aloud for understanding,
And if you look for it as for silver and search for it as for
Hidden treasure, then you will understand the fear
Of the Lord and find the knowledge of God.

Proverbs 2:1-7

Godly Wisdom in the Affairs of Life

Father, You said if anyone lacks wisdom, let him ask of You, and it shall be given him. Therefore, I ask in faith, nothing wavering, to be filled with the knowledge of Your will in all wisdom and spiritual understanding. Today I incline my ear unto wisdom, and I apply my heart to understanding so that I might receive that which has been freely given unto me.

In the name of Jesus, I receive skill and Godly wisdom and instruction. I discern and comprehend the words of understanding and insight. I receive instruction in wise dealing and the discipline of wise thoughtfulness, righteousness, justice, and integrity. Prudence, knowledge, discretion, and discernment are given to me. I increase in knowledge. As a person of understanding, I acquire skill and attain to sound counsels so that I may be able to steer my course rightly.

Therefore, I will walk in paths of uprightness. When I walk, my steps shall not be hampered—my path will be clear and open; and when I run, I shall not stumble. I take fast hold of instruction and do not let her go; I guard her, for she is my life. I let my eyes look right on, with fixed purpose, and my gaze is straight before me. I consider well the path of my feet, and let all my ways be established and ordered aright.

Father, in the name of Jesus, I look carefully to how I walk! I live purposefully and worthily and accurately, not as unwise and witless, but as a wise—sensible, intelligent—person, making the very most of my time—buying up every opportunity. In Jesus' name. Amen.

Scripture References

Colossians 1:9   Colossians 2:3
Proverbs 2:2   Proverbs 2:7
Proverbs 1:2-52   Corinthians 5:21

But if anyone does not provide for his own,
And especially for those of his household,
He has denied the faith,
And is worse than an unbeliever.

1 Timothy 5:8

Family Second

A man must leave his father and mother
When he marries, so that he can be perfectly joined
To his wife, and the two shall be one.

Ephesians 5:31

My Wife and Marriage

Father, in the beginning, You provided a partner for man. Now I have found a wife to be my partner, and I have obtained favor from the Lord.

In the name of Jesus, I purpose to provide leadership to my wife the way Christ does to His church, not by domineering, but by cherishing. I will go all out in my love for her, exactly as Christ did for the Church—a love marked by giving, not getting. We are the Body of Christ, and when I love my wife, I love myself.

It is my desire to give my wife what is due her, and I purpose to share my personal rights with her. Father, I am neither anxious nor intimidated, but I am a good husband to my wife. I honor her and delight in her. In the new life of God's Grace, we are equals. I purpose to treat my wife as an equal so that our prayers will be answered.

We bear up under anything and everything that comes. We are ever ready to believe the best of each other. Our hopes are fadeless under all circumstances. We endure everything without weakening. Our love never fails—it never fades out or becomes obsolete or comes to an end.

We are no longer children tossed to and fro, carried about with every wind of doctrine, but we speak the truth in love, dealing truly and living truly. We are enfolded in love, growing up in every way and in all things. We esteem and delight in one another, forgiving one another readily and freely as God in Christ has forgiven us. We are imitators of God and copy His example as well-beloved children imitate their father.

Thank You, Father, that our marriage grows stronger each day because it is founded on Your Word and on Your kind of love. We give You the praise for it all, Father, in the name of Jesus, Amen. (*Add any specific prayers you have for your wife.*)

Scripture References

Matthew 18:18   Ephesians 5:22, 23
Genesis 2:18   1 Corinthians 7:3-5
Proverbs 18:22   1 Peter 3:9

Houses and wealth are inherited from parents

But a prudent wife is from the Lord.

Proverbs 19:14

Single Male Trusting God for a Mate

Father, in the name of Jesus, I believe that You are providing a suitable helpmate for me. According to Your Word, she will adapt herself to me, respect, honor, prefer, esteem me and stand firmly by my side. She will be united in spirit and purpose, having the same love and being in full accord and of one harmonious mind and intention.

Father, You say in Your Word that a wise, understanding, and prudent wife is from You. He who finds a true wife finds a good thing and obtains favor of You.

Father, I know that I have found favor in Your sight, and I praise You and thank You for Your Word, knowing that You watch over it to perform it. Amen.

Scripture References

Ephesians 5:22, 23   Philippians 2:2
Proverbs 18:22   Jeremiah 1:12

Children are a gift from God; they are His reward.

Children born to a young man are like sharp arrows

To defend him. Happy is the man who

Has his quiver full of them.

Psalm 127:3-5

My Children

Father, in the name of Jesus, I pray and confess Your Word over my children, _____, and surround them with my faith — faith in Your Word that You watch over it to perform it! I confess and believe that my children are Disciples of Christ, taught of the Lord and obedient to Your will. Great is the peace and undisturbed composure of my children, because You, God, contend with that which contends with my children, and You give them safety and ease them.

Father, you will perfect that which concerns me. I commit that all may be well with my children and that they may live long on earth, for You are their Life and the Length of their days. I cast the care of my children once and for all over on You, Father. They are in Your hands, and I am positively persuaded that You are able to guard and keep that which I have committed to You. You are more than enough!

I believe and confess that You give Your angels charge over my children to accompany and defend and preserve them in all their ways. You, Lord, are their Refuge and Fortress. You protect them from the enemy. You are their Glory and the Lifter of their heads.

As a father, I will not provoke, irritate, or fret my children. I will not be hard on them or harass them or cause them to become discouraged, sullen, or morose, or to feel inferior and frustrated. I will not break or wound their spirits, but I will rear them tenderly in the training, discipline, counsel, and admonition of the Lord. I will train them in the way they should go, and when they are old, they will not depart from it. Thank you, Father, for caring for my children. In Jesus' name, Amen. *(Add any specific prayers you may have for your children.)*

Scripture References

Jeremiah 1:12	Psalm 91:11
Isaiah 54:13	Psalm 91:2
Isaiah 49:25	Psalm 3:3
1 Peter 5:7	Colossians 3:21
2 Timothy 1:12	

The generation of the upright will be blessed.

Wealth and riches are in His house,

And His righteousness endures forever.

Psalm 112:1-2

Blessing the Household

Father, as the priest and head of this household, I declare and decree, "As for me and my house, we shall serve the Lord."

Lord, we acknowledge and welcome the presence of Your Holy Spirit here in our home. We thank You Father, that Your Son, Jesus, is here with us because we are gathered together in His name.

As spiritual leader of this home, I declare on the authority of Your Word that my family will be mighty in the land; this generation of the upright will be blessed.

Father, You delight in the prosperity of Your people and we thank You for the blessings in our house and that our righteousness endures forever, in the name of Jesus, Amen.

Scripture References

Revelation 1:6	Matthew 18:20
Joshua 24:15	2 Peter 1:3
Ephesians 1:3	Psalm 112:2
John 4:23	Psalm 112:3

And God is able to make all grace abound to you,

So that in all things at all times,

Having all that you need, you will abound

In every good work. As it is written:

"He has scattered abroad His gifts to the poor;

His righteousness endures forever."

2 Corinthians 9:8-9

Handling Household Finances

Jesus, you are my Lord and my High Priest, and I purpose to bring You the first fruits of my income and worship You, the Lord my God, with them. Therefore, I believe in the name of Jesus that all my needs are met, according to Your riches in glory. I acknowledge You as Lord over my finances by giving tithes and offerings to further Your cause.

> If you've not been giving tithes and offerings, include the following in your prayer: Forgive me for robbing you in the tithes and offerings. I repent and purpose to bring all my tithes into the storehouse that there may be food in your house. Thank you for wise financial counselors and teachers who are teaching me the principles of good stewardship.

Father, on the authority of Your Word, I declare that gifts will be given to me; good measure, pressed down, shaken together, and running over shall they be poured into my bosom. For with the same measure I deal out, it shall be measured back to me.

I remember that it is written in Your Word that he who sows sparingly and grudgingly, will also reap sparingly and grudgingly. He who sows generously that blessings may come to someone, will also reap generously and with blessings.

Father, not only do I give tithes and offerings to You, but I also give to those around me who are in need. Your Word also says that he who gives to the poor lends to You, and You pay wonderful interest on the loan! I acknowledge You as I give for the benefit of the poor.

Thank You, Father, that as You bless me and I bless others, they will praise You and give You thanks. They will bless others and the circle of Your love and blessings will go on and on into eternity, in the name of Jesus, Amen. (*Add specific prayers for your own financial needs.*)

Scripture References

John 14:17	Isaiah 55:11
Hebrews 3:1	Proverbs 19:17
Philippians 4:19	Luke 6:38

I will instruct you and teach you in the way
You should go; I will counsel you and
Watch over you.
Psalm 32:8

Career Third

Whatever you do, work at it with all your heart,

As working for the Lord, not for men, since you know that

You will receive an inheritance from the Lord as a reward.

It is the Lord Christ you are serving.

Colossians 3:23-24

The Setting of Proper Priorities

Father, too often I allow urgency to dictate my schedule, and I am asking You to help me establish priorities in my work. My desire is to live purposefully, worthily, accurately as a wise, sensible, intelligent person.

You have given me a seven-day week — six days to work and the seventh day to rest. I desire to make the most of the time buying up each opportunity. Help me plan my day, and stay focused on my assignments. Help me to organize my efforts, schedule my activities and budget my time.

By the grace given me, I will not worry about missing out, and my everyday human concerns will be met. I purpose in my heart to seek first of all Your Kingdom, Lord, and Your righteousness, and then all things taken together will be given me.

Father, Your Word is my compass, and it helps me see my life as complete in Christ. I cast all my cares, worries and concerns on You, that I might be well-balanced, temperate, sober of mind, vigilant and cautious at all times.

Father, You sent Jesus that I might have life and have it more abundantly. Help me remember that my relationship with You and with others are more important than anything else. In the name of Jesus. Amen.

Scripture References

Ephesians 5:15, 16   Genesis 2:2
Proverbs 16:3, 9   John 10:10
Colossians 2:10   1 Peter 5:7, 8
Matthew 11:29   Proverbs 2:3

But remember the Lord your God,

For it is He who gives you the ability to produce wealth,

And so confirms His covenant,

Which He swore to your forefathers, as it is today.

Deuteronomy 8:18

Prayer for the Success of Business
(Only if you are self employed)

Father, I commit my works (the plans and cares of my business) to You, I entrust them wholly to You. Since You are effectually at work in me, You cause my thoughts to become agreeable with Your will, so that my business plans shall be established and will succeed. In the name of Jesus, I submit to every kind of wisdom, practical insight, and prudence, which You have lavished upon me in accordance with the riches and generosity of Your gracious favor.

Father, I affirm that I obey Your Word by making an honest living with my own hands, so that I may be able to give to those in need. In Your strength and according to Your grace, I provide for myself and my own family. Thank You, Father, for making all grace, every favor and earthly blessing, come to me in abundance that I, having all sufficiency may abound to every good work.

Thank You for the grace to remain diligent in seeking knowledge and skill in areas where I am inexperienced. I ask You for wisdom and the ability to understand righteousness, justice, and fair dealing in every area and relationship. I affirm that I am faithful and committed to Your Word. My life and business are founded upon its principles.

Father, thank You for the success of my business! In Jesus' name, Amen.

Scripture References

Romans 8:17	1 Timothy 5:8
Colossians 1:12	Hebrews 1:14
Philemon 1:6	Matthew 5:14, 16
Proverbs 16:3	Proverbs 22:29
Philippians 2:13	Proverbs 2:9
Ephesians 1:7, 8	Proverbs 4:20-22

If you're a hard worker and do a good job,
You deserve your pay; we don't call your wages a gift.
But if you see that the job is too big for you,
That it's something only God can do,
And you trust Him to do it, you could never
Do it for yourself, no matter how hard and long
You worked. Well, that trusting-Him-to-do-it is what
Gets you set right with God by God. Sheer gift.

Romans 4:4-5

Prayer for Personal Productivity on the Job
(If You Are Employed)

Father, I ask for Your help in planning my day, paying attention to my duties, staying focused on my assignment, establishing priorities in my work, and making steady progress toward my objectives.

Give me insight, Father. Help me to see any habits that I may have that might tend to make me nonproductive. Reveal to me ways to better handle the tedious tasks I must perform so that I can achieve the greatest results possible. Help me to organize my efforts, schedule my activities, and budget my time.

From books, by Your Spirit, through the people who work with me or by whatever means You choose, Lord, reveal to me that which I need to know and do in order to become a more productive, fruitful worker.

My heart's desire is to give my very best to You and to my employer. When I become frustrated because that is not taking place, help me, Father by the power of Your Spirit to do whatever is necessary to correct that situation so that I can once again function with accuracy and proficiency.

Thank You, Lord, for bringing all these things to pass in my life. In Jesus' name I pray, Amen. (*Add specific prayers for your personal challenges.*)

Scripture References

Psalm 118:24   Psalm 119:99
Proverbs 16:9   Proverbs 9:10
Ephesians 1:17

Watch the way you talk…
Say only what helps, each word a gift…
Be gentle with one another, sensitive.
Forgive one another as quickly and thoroughly
As God in Christ forgave you.
Ephesians 4:29, 32

Improving Communication Skills

Father, I am Your child, Jesus said that if I pray to You in secret, You will reward me openly. Show "me" to me. Uncover me and bring everything to the light. When anything is exposed by the light, it is made visible and clear; and where everything is visible and clear, there is light.

Teach me to speak the truth in love in my home, in my church, with my friends, and in all my relationships. Words are powerful. The power of life and death is in the tongue, and You said that I would eat the fruit of it. Father, I realize that words can be creative or destructive. A word out of my mouth may seem of no account, but it can accomplish nearly anything — or destroy it.

With the help of the Holy Spirit and by Your grace, I will not let any unwholesome talk come out of my mouth, but only what is helpful for building others up according to their needs, that it may benefit those who listen, in Jesus' name, Amen.

Scripture References

1 John 3:1	Ephesians 4:29
Matthew 6:6	Psalm 45:1
Hebrews 11:6	Proverbs 3:3
Ephesians 5:13	Proverbs 8:6-8
Proverbs 4:23	Proverbs 10:20, 21
Ephesians 4:15	Proverbs 31:26

The first thing I want you to do is pray.
Pray every way you know how, for everyone you know.
Pray especially for rulers and their governments
To rule well so we can be quietly about our business
Of living simply, in humble contemplation.
This is the way our Savior God wants us to live.

1 Timothy 2:1-3

Prayer for the President and Our Nation

Father, in Jesus' name, I give thanks for the United States and its government. I hold up in prayer before You the men and women who are in positions of authority.

I pray that skillful and Godly wisdom will enter into the heart of our president and knowledge is pleasant to him. May discretion watch over him; may understanding keep him and deliver him from the way of evil and from evil men.

Your Word declares that "blessed is the nation whose God is the Lord." We receive Your blessing. Father, You are our Refuge and Stronghold. I declare that Your people dwell safely in this land, and prosper abundantly. We are all more than conquerors through Christ Jesus!

It is written in Your Word that the heart of our President is in the hand of the Lord and that You turn it whichever way You desire. I pray that You put the heart of our President in Your hands Father, and from this day forward that all his decisions will be divinely directed by You.

I give thanks unto You that the good news of the Gospel is published in our land. I pray that The Word of the Lord prevails and grows mightily in the hearts and lives of the American people. I give thanks for this land and the leaders You have given to us, in Jesus' name we pray, Amen.

Scripture References

1 Timothy 2:1-3	Deuteronomy 28:10, 11
Proverbs 2:10-12, 21, 22	Romans 8:37
Psalm 33:12	Proverbs 21:1
Psalm 9:9	Acts 12:24

It is good to praise the Lord and make music to Your Name,

O Most High, to proclaim Your love in the morning

And your faithfulness at night.

Psalm 92:1-2

To Glorify God

In view of God's mercy, I offer my body as a living sacrifice, holy and pleasing to God—this is my spiritual act of worship. It is not in my own strength; for it is You, Lord, who are all the while effectually at work in me. You are energizing and creating in me the power and desire—both to will and work for Your good pleasure and satisfaction and delight.

Father, I will not draw back or shrink in fear, for then Your soul would have no delight or pleasure in me. I was bought for a price—purchased with a preciousness and paid for, made Your very own. So, then, I honor You Lord, and bring glory to You in my body. I called on You in the day of trouble; You delivered me. I shall honor and glorify You. I rejoice because You delivered me and drew me to Yourself. You took me out of the control and dominion of darkness, obscurity, and transferred me into the Kingdom of the Son of Your love. I will confess and praise You, O Lord my God, with my whole, united heart. I will glorify Your name forever.

As a bond servant of Jesus Christ, I receive and develop the talents that have been given me, for I would have You say of me, "Well done, you upright and faithful servant!" I make use of the gifts (faculties, talents, qualities) according to the grace given me. I let my light shine before men that they may see my moral excellence and my praiseworthy, noble and good deeds. I recognize, honor, praise and glorify my Father Who is in heaven.

In the name of Jesus, I allow my life to lovingly express truth in all things—speaking truly, dealing truly and living truly. Whatever I do, no matter what it is—in word or deed, I do everything in the name of the Lord Jesus Christ. My dependence is upon His Person, giving praise to God the Father through Him.

Whatever may be my task, I work at it heartily from the soul, as something done for the Lord and not for men. To God the Father be all glory, honor and praise. In the name of Jesus. Amen

Scripture References

Romans 12:1
Philippians 2:13

Matthew 25:2
Romans 12:6

NOTES

photographing
Maui

Where to Find Perfect Shots and How to Take Them

Douglas Peebles

THE COUNTRYMAN PRESS
WOODSTOCK, VERMONT

To my wife, Margaret, who is still trying to figure out when to go with me and when to send me out on my own.

Maps by Paul Woodward, © The Countryman Press
Book design and composition by S. E. Livingston

Photographing Maui
978-0-88150-937-3

Published by The Countryman Press,
P.O. Box 748, Woodstock, VT 05091

Distributed by W. W. Norton & Company, Inc.,
500 Fifth Avenue, New York, NY 10110

Printed in the United States of America

10 9 8 7 6 5 4 3 2 1

Title Page: Sunset in Kihei
Right: Lahaina

Acknowledgments

I came to Hawaii in 1974 and made my first trip to Maui that year. Since then I have been to Maui over 100 times. Many people have helped me along the way. Some whose names I have forgotten and others I am afraid I will forget to mention.

First to thank is Bennet Hymer. I have done several Maui book projects with him over the years and enjoyed every one. I have also had the pleasure of working with Peter Cannon, Ursula Mahoney, Larry Blieberg, Kristen Shelton, Lane Gregory, Jill Supka, Maggie Perkins, Joyce Timpson, Robert Glick, and others I know I am failing to list.

While on Maui I have had the help of many friends and associates. These include Carl Lindquist, Dave Sheetz, Darrell Wong, Chuck Whiteman, Bob Lee, Sheila Donnelly, Keli'I Brown, and Bruce (I thought you had the tripod) Nagel.

Finally, I want to thank Kim Grant, who both got me into this project and got me through it.

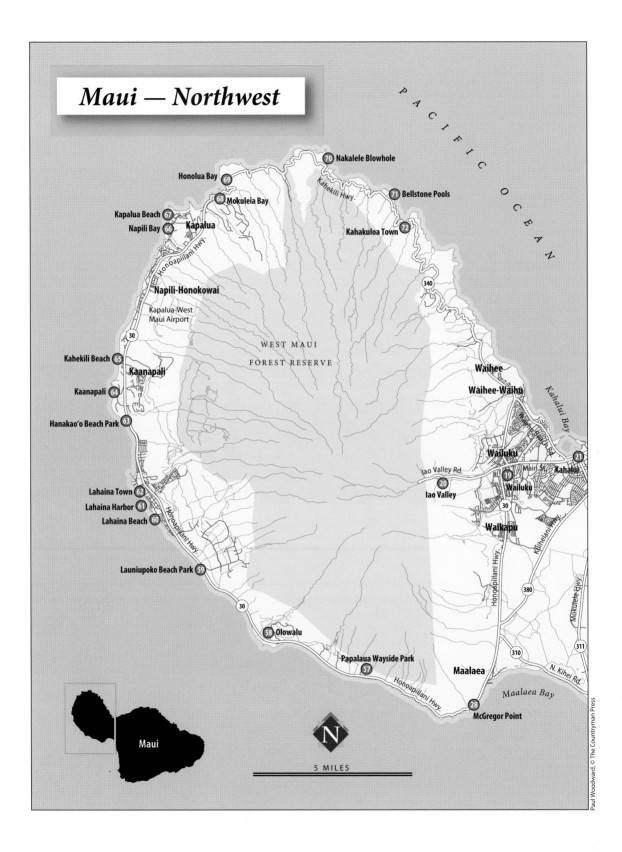

Maui — Northwest

PACIFIC OCEAN

70 Nakalele Blowhole

Honolua Bay 69

71 Bellstone Pools

68 Mokuleia Bay

Kapalua Beach 67
Kapalua
Napili Bay 66

72 Kahakuloa Town

Kahekili Hwy.

Napili-Honokowai

Kapalua-West
Maui Airport

340

WEST MAUI
FOREST RESERVE

Kahekili Beach 65

Waihee

Waihee-Waihu

Kaanapali

Kaanapali 64

Kahalui Bay

Hanakao'o Beach Park 63

Wailuku

Iao Valley Rd.
21
Main St.
Kahalui

Lahaina Town 62
Lahaina Harbor 61
Lahaina Beach 60

19
Wailuku

20
Iao Valley

30

Honoapiilani Hwy.

Waikapu

Launiupoko Beach Park 59

Honoapiilani Hwy.

380

30

Mokulele Hwy.

58 Olowalu

310

311

Papalaua Wayside Park
57

Maalaea

N. Kihei Rd.

Honoapiilani Hwy.

Maalaea Bay

28
McGregor Point

Maui

N

5 MILES

Paul Woodward, © The Countryman Press

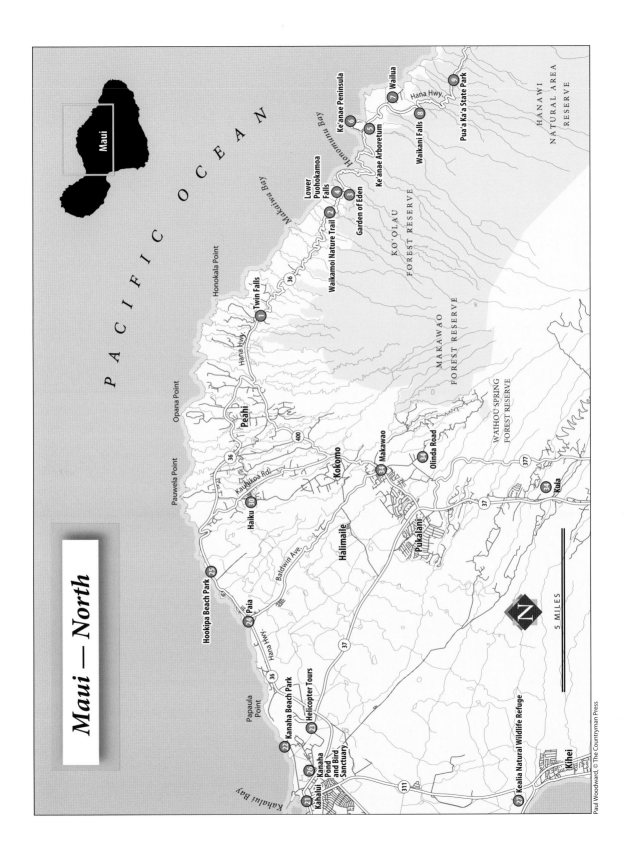

Maui — North

PACIFIC OCEAN

Maui

HANAWI
NATURAL AREA
RESERVE

9 Pua'a Ka'a State Park

7 Wailua
Hana Hwy.
8 Waikani Falls

Ke'anae Peninsula
6
5
Ke'anae Arboretum

Honomanu Bay

KO'OLAU
FOREST RESERVE

Lower
Puohokamoa
Falls
2 4
3 Garden of Eden
Waikamoi Nature Trail

Makiawa Bay

Honokala Point

36

MAKAWAO
FOREST RESERVE

Twin Falls
1

Hana Hwy.

Opana Point

Peãhi

WAIHOU SPRING
FOREST RESERVE

400

36

Makawao
31 34 Olinda Road

Pauwela Point

Kaupikoa Rd.

Kokomo

377

Haiku
10

Baldwin Ave.

Pukalani

37

32 Kula

Pauaula Point

Hookipa Beach Park
25

Halimaile

24 Paia

Hana Hwy.

37

N
5 MILES

Papaula Point

Kanaha Beach Park
23 Helicopter Tours
22
26 Kanaha Pond
and Bird
Sanctuary

311

Kealia Natural Wildlife Refuge
27

Kahului

Kihei

Kahului Bay

Paul Woodward, © The Countryman Press

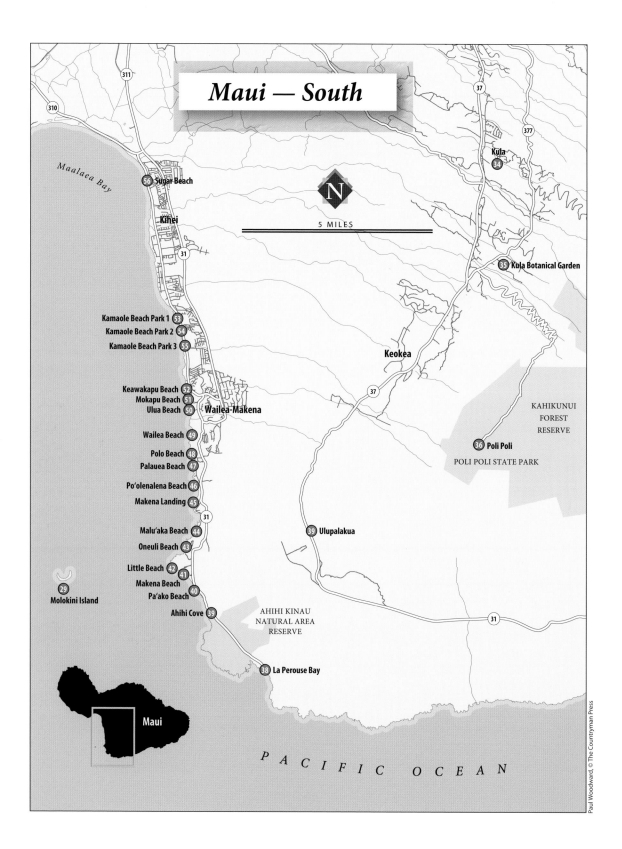

Maui — South

Maalaea Bay

56 Sugar Beach

Kihei

Kula 34

Kula Botanical Garden 35

5 MILES

N

Kamaole Beach Park 1 53
Kamaole Beach Park 2 54
Kamaole Beach Park 3 55

Keokea

Keawakapu Beach 52
Mokapu Beach 51
Ulua Beach 50   Wailea-Makena

KAHIKUNUI
FOREST
RESERVE

Wailea Beach 49

Polo Beach 48
Palauea Beach 47

36 Poli Poli

POLI POLI STATE PARK

Po'olenalena Beach 46

Makena Landing 45

Malu'aka Beach 44

Oneuli Beach 43

39 Ulupalakua

Little Beach 42
41
Makena Beach
Pa'ako Beach 40

29
Molokini Island

Ahihi Cove 39

AHIHI KINAU
NATURAL AREA
RESERVE

31

Maui

38 La Perouse Bay

P A C I F I C   O C E A N

Paul Woodward, © The Countryman Press

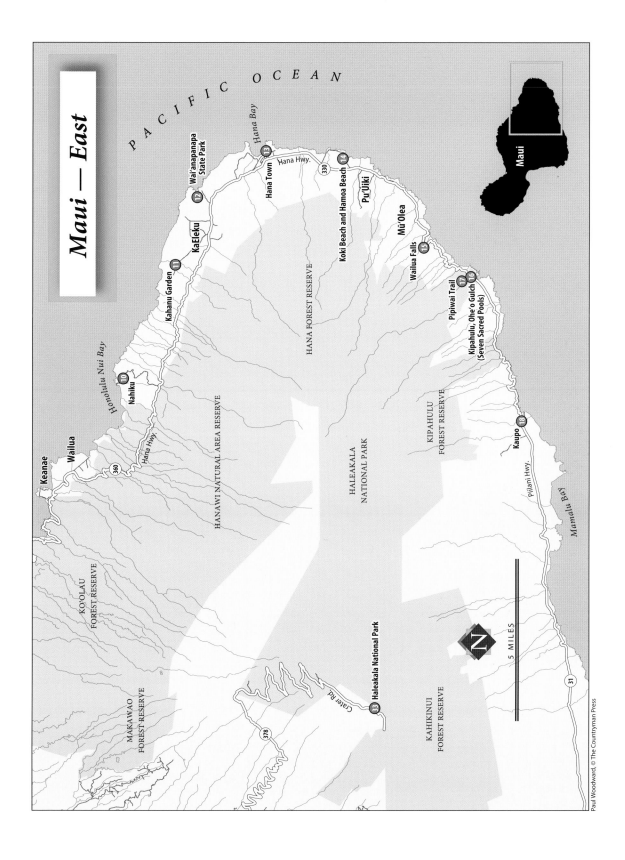

Maui — East

PACIFIC OCEAN

Hana Bay

Wai'anapanapa State Park
13
Hana Town
Hana Hwy.
330
12
Ka Eleku
14
Pu'Uiki
Koki Beach and Hamoa Beach
Kahanu Garden
11
Mū'Olea
Honolulu Nui Bay
Wailua Falls
15
17
Pipiwai Trail
16
Kipahulu, Ohe'o Gulch
(Seven Sacred Pools)
HANA FOREST RESERVE
Nahiku
10
HANAWI NATURAL AREA RESERVE
KIPAHULU FOREST RESERVE
Keanae
Wailua
360
Hana Hwy.
Kaupo
Pilani Hwy.
HALEAKALA NATIONAL PARK
Mamalu Bay
KOYOLAU FOREST RESERVE
N
5 MILES
KAHIKINUI FOREST RESERVE
MAKAWAO FOREST RESERVE
Crater Rd.
23
Haleakala National Park
378
31

Maui

Paul Woodward, © The Countryman Press

The road to Haleakala

Contents

Honolua Bay

Maui rates at the top among the world's scenic places. Mountains plunge into a sea edged with black lava rock and spray-crested wild waves. Deep valleys cut into the mountains like the arrangement in a Chinese painting. Sunsets on West and South Maui streak the sky scarlet, hot pink, cool mauve and lavender.

Everyone wants to take home memories of these scenes. Prints or slide shows of palm-fringed Napīli Bay, a Lahaina sunset, Hana Road waterfalls, or a Kula protea blossom conjure up the soft air and the breathtaking beauty.

Douglas Peebles, the photographer-writer of this book, is eminently qualified to guide us to Maui's most scenic spots. A Hawaii resident, he has provided photographs for 50 books on the state over the course of more than 25 years. His books explore the island's large scale, including his aerial images for the From the Skies of Paradise series about the Hawaiian Islands. He reveals the hidden corners in books such as the Majesty series on exceptional trees, and *Pua Nani* on Hawaiian gardens. His distinctive images also appear regularly in national magazines, ads, annual reports, and other publications.

In this guide, the award-winning travel photographer identifies the top scenic spots in each of Maui's five major regions. He gives precise locations, tells you how to get there, and recommends viewpoints for the camera. He offers some professional tips, but the book is aimed at the point-and-shoot casual photographer as well as the person with the digital SLR and a battery of lenses. Sometimes he cautions you where not to go out of respect for local residents or for reasons of safety.

Peebles shares the aesthetics of photographing this unique island. He writes that color, content, and composition guide him. These ideas underlie his choices and advice.

Even Maui's shape, a lopsided figure 8 created by two separate volcanic events, adds interest to landscape photography. Anywhere from West and South Maui you'll see other islands, Molokai and Lanai or Kahoolawe and Molokini, which form spectacular silhouettes against the sunsets.

The color spectrum is astonishing. The sea ranges from pale aqua at the shore to deep sapphire at the horizon. The Hana Coast has more shades of green than you'll find on a paint chart. Punctuating the green are the red blossoms of the African tulip trees and, if you venture to Haleakala's foothills, the brilliant plumage of the apapane bird.

People leave their mark on this landscape, from the plantation-era board buildings to the missionary churches and, from the more distant past, the massive Piilanihale Heiau near Hana.

Peebles knows all of Maui's richness and opens it up for the visitor. Even if you don't photograph, you'll see more for using his book.

—Carol Fowler, Author of *Great Destinations Hawaii: Maui*

Protea

How to Use This Book

F8 and be there! If you have been into scenic or landscape photography for very long you have probably heard that "F8 and be there" is the number one rule. It's true. Being at the right place at the right time vastly improves your photographs. It's been said that if you want to be famous for photographing beautiful people then start by photographing beautiful people. It makes it a lot easier.

The trick to photographing beautiful landscapes though is finding the right place at the right time. That's what this book is about. Maui is an incredible island. It has been voted, over a dozen times, Best Island in the World by the readers of *Condé Nast Traveler* magazine. It's not hard to find good spots to photograph. The purpose of the book is to help you find the best spots when they are most beautiful. I hope it will make your photography a lot easier.

Maui is not a very large island. It's 729 square miles (Rhode Island is 1,214 square miles). It's 48 miles long and 26 miles across at it's widest. You can get anywhere and back in a day. Planning a day for photography would seem simple, but in some ways it's not. Because of the irregular shape of the island, the sweep of the bays, and the height of the mountains, the sun is not always where you think it might be. There are some dramatic sunsets that can be seen from the east side of the island. On the south side sometimes the sun does not clear Haleakala till almost 10 A.M.

I have divided the island into five areas: the Hana Coast, West Maui, South Maui, Central Maui, and Haleakala and Upcountry. This does not mean you should do them in any order. Most any day trip will take you through two or three of these regions. All of the locations listed in this book are easy to get to. There are no long hikes or four- wheel-drive vehicles needed. In a few cases there may be some short climbing to get the best angle or view. I will point those out, and discretion and caution are advised.

There will be some other cautions as needed, but Maui is generally a very safe place. Sunscreen, a good pair of shoes, and water are usually all you need. I will also include helpful pro tips. These will either be technical pointers on lenses, filters, and such or creative suggestions on composition, content, or timing.

You will also find diversions throughout the book—things to see or do in the area. They may not be photographic opportunities but could be of interest to you or someone you're traveling with. Traveling with a photographer is sometimes not that much fun, or so I have been told, several times actually. Your companion may not share you enthusiasm for standing on the beach for an hour waiting to get the clouds just right. Some of these ideas might help.

One last thing to keep in mind is that this book is a guide, but it's only a guide. Be flexible and keep your eyes open, and I am sure you'll find opportunities that are not listed here. For me that's the most exciting photography: either shooting in a new place or finding new images in a spot I have been before. I hope with this book, a map, and your camera gear you'll get out and enjoy the island. Actually I'm sure you will. You are in Maui!

Haleakala, Maui

How I Photograph Maui

The hardware and mechanics are easy to explain. I photograph with a digital camera, a professional 35mm full-frame single lens reflex to be specific. I also carry several lenses, filters, and a tripod. Usually I will have a minimum of three lenses—16–35mm, 24–105mm, and 70–200mm—in my backpack. These are also all professional equipment. That means they are both expensive and heavy. I will also have a tripod, a polarizing filter and a neutral density graduated filter. I really wish I could get by with something easier. I do have a great pocket-size digital camera with an incredibly sharp 24–85mm equivalent lens. I could use that for 90 percent of what I shoot but the results would not be quite as good.

However, either camera setup will work for the photo guidelines given in this book. While I will sometimes note what specific gear I am carrying or using, this will not be a step-by-step photography course. I hope to be able to make as many aesthetic suggestions as technical ones. For me the most important aesthetic considerations are color, content and composition.

Content, Composition, and Color

Content

Deciding what to photograph is the first and most important step. Most of this book deals with scenic/landscape photography but the process is the same regardless of what the subject is. Whatever your subject is it should be something you love to shoot. I know photographers who specialize only in surfing, whales, windsurfing, underwater, kiteboarding, and hula dancing. All of that and more can be found on Maui. The more you know about your subject, the more research you do before you go out, the better your photos will be.

I will go online to research an area I am interested in. I no longer need to in Maui but for other places I will get a guidebook and a map. I will look online for photos of the area to see what has been done. Lately I have been using Google Earth to preview some locations. It's amazing the detail that can be seen there, especially along the coastlines. Sometimes, if it's a long or complicated trip, I will make a shot list. I can never truly follow it as written, but it feels good to cross items off. It also helps in planning while on the road. All of this helps me define or refine my content.

Composition

Composition in photography is all about squeezing a three-dimensional world onto a two dimensional plane. Some choices are technical, such as what lens, what shutter speed and the amount of depth of field/focus. These affect your composition as much as the aesthetic

The West Maui Mountains

choices of angle of view, framing, or cropping might. I always have a good idea of what I am after before I lift the camera to my eye. Generally I am trying to include a foreground, middle ground, and background into every photo. This maintains the feel of a 3D world. The middle ground is most often the subject. One example of this might be a beach with someone on it, framed by palm trees, with a cliff in the background. Here the palms and cliff give depth even if all are in focus. Another example might be a red protea flower with some out of focus foliage in the foreground and black space in the back. Here it's the shallow depth of focus, only on the flower, that gives it depth. Also, in this photo, the choice and position of the background is just as important as the middle ground/subject. The background is so important that often I will start my composition with it.

There are a number of guidelines to creative composition, such as the rule of thirds, leading diagonal lines, or use of depth of field. These are best studied through courses, workshops, or books. A publication such as *The Basic Book of Digital Photography* by Michelle and Tom Grimm is a good place to start. A lot of it can be learned that way, but much of it is truly instinctive, and some people will never get it.

One quick step that can greatly improve your compositions is to do an immediate review of what you have just done. To me this is one of the biggest advantages of digital photography. I am always taking a look at the back of my camera to study how the shot looks in 2D. I check to see if there is a better way to line up the foreground or background. I look for distractions that I did not see with my eyes, like utility lines or trash on the ground. When I look at the scene with my eyes I often filter those things out but they stand out in an image. With film often I would not see them till I was back in my office. Now I catch most of them in the field.

Color

The predominant colors of Maui are blue and green. You will be seeing a lot of blue and green, but that is not what I mean by color. I am talking about the use of color as a photographic element. Should you intensify those blues and greens through polarization or postproduction saturation? That will certainly make you photos bolder. You could go the other route and shoot everything through yellow, brown, or orange warming filters. That can give a calming, sometimes nostalgic feeling to scenes. Or you could dispense with color all together and shoot black and white. That can work well in tropical gardens or along rocky coastlines. All of these are creative color choices that you need to make.

I always shoot in color, and many of these choices I now make in the postproduction process. I do look for strong colors on location though. On Maui I am often searching for reds or yellows to contrast against the blues and greens. This can be found in sailboats or windsurfers against the ocean or sky. It could be a red orchid in a green garden or rainforest. It's really just a question, or maybe quest, of finding the elements and arranging them as best you can.

Light and weather, rain or shine

Of course it's the weather that will be the biggest determining factor on what elements you can find or use for your photography. Fortunately you'll be on Maui, and while the weather won't always be perfect, it is very rarely so bad that it will shut you down. You really can shoot rain or shine.

Generally when it's sunny I head to the coast to photograph the beaches, bays, and shorelines. These are most beautiful during the golden hours, which are the two hours before

A waterfall in Hana

sunset, or after sunrise. However in Hawaii the water is bluer in the middle of the day. This means great shots, especially of the beaches and of surfing or sailing, can be done all day.

Cloudy days I head for the mountains. Clouds mean soft, even light, which is perfect for streams, waterfalls, rainforests, and botanical gardens. I enjoy cloudy days. I grab my camera, tripod, telephoto or macro lens, water, bug spray, and maybe an umbrella. Light is still better either early or late in the day but you can still shoot at noon, especially close-ups.

You do need to be careful around streams when it's raining. Flash floods do happen, and people have been washed away.

Sunrise, sunset

The good news is that there really aren't that many good places to shoot the sunrise on Maui.

That means you can sleep in. The biggest exception is Haleakala, and you will have to get up very, very early in the morning to catch that one. There are a couple of spots on the Hana Coast that are beautiful at sunrise as well.

There are a lot of opportunities for stunning sunsets though. Along the whole coastline from Makena through Wailea, Kihei, and Ma'alea you can see the sun go down into the ocean or behind Kahoolawe. From Olowalu through Lahaina, Kaanapali, Napili, and Kapalua you see much of the same with Lanai or Molokai in the background.

I will photograph sunsets with every lens from a super-wide-angle to my longest telephoto (16mm–400mm). I use a tripod for all lenses. I rarely put on special filters anymore because I can do that in postproduction. Often I will stay up to 30 minutes past sunset to catch the afterglow of twilight. This works very well on calm days, and it's amazing what you can get now with digital cameras. Try to keep shooting even when you think it's too dark. The camera will see more than you can.

Photographic equipment

All of my cameras are now digital. So all of my technical suggestions and many of my creative ones will be assuming that you're working with a digital camera as well. I believe digital photography has too many advantages over film for anyone to willingly stay behind. Its quality has surpassed 35mm film, especially on any ISO speeds past 100. The automatic white balance makes it easy to photograph anyplace inside, outside, or any time of day. The instant review gives both information and confidence to the photographer. And finally it's a much more green process. There are no longer thousands of gallons of developing chemicals and silver halides flowing into our water supply.

Right now I have three full-frame digital SLR cameras, and at any given time I will usually have two of them with me. I have lenses from 15mm to 400mm but am most often in the field with three zooms—16–35mm, 24–105mm, and 70–200mm—and a 100mm macro squeezed in. I have a light backpacking tripod and a slightly heavier one I use when I

Sunrise in Keʻanae

know I will be staying relatively close to the car. I always recommend using a tripod!

The problem with that tripod advice is I don't always follow it myself. I will often get out of the car with just one camera and one lens, the 16–35mm for beach coastlines or the 24–105mm for towns. This works well for me. It frees my mind to concentrate on the subject and not on my gear.

Throughout this book I will be making some references to what gear I am using. Mainly I will be talking about which lenses, for it's the lenses, not the cameras, which really make the photograph. It's much easier to see the difference between a wide and normal lens, than between a Nikon and a Canon camera.

Other items to carry

Sunscreen, water, and a good pair of shoes should be at the top of everybody's list. I have a cell phone and a whistle for emergencies. I always take an umbrella or a cheap plastic poncho for rain.

Photographically there isn't as much as there used to be in my bag. Because there's so much that can be done in processing digital files, I now only carry two filters. Those are a polarizer and a graduated grey neutral density. The polarizer is good for reflections and intensifying blues and greens on sunny or cloudy days. You have to be careful with it because it's easy to overdo, especially with wide-angle lenses. I don't use it as much as I did with film.

The graduated neutral density I use is an ND6, which has a three-stop gradation. Its effect can be created in post-processing, but it's much better to use it at exposure. It's very helpful for some sunsets and mountain scenes where the foreground is dark. Extra batteries, extra memory cards, and a cable release for the camera are the only other items in the backpack.

Makena Beach

Potential problems

There really are not a whole lot of potential problems in Maui. You don't have to wear bells to warn bears. I moved here from Florida, so one of my favorite things about Hawaii is that you do not have to worry about snakes. There are none. You can cut through the bushes without a care. There is no poison ivy or poison

A panoramic view of the Keʻanae Peninsula

oak. However, the place in not totally without hazards, therefore you should not think sunburn is your only risk and be totally oblivious to everything else.

Getting lost

Getting lost is one of them. It's surprisingly easy to get sidetracked, to get off the trail to take a photo, or to take the wrong fork on the way back. I have done it a few times. Once I was lost in what seemed to be a gigantic bamboo forest above Kipahulu. After many hours, just before dark, I stumbled out. That is why I now always have a cell phone and a whistle.

Streams

Except for the ocean, streams are the most dangerous part of Maui: You can slip, you can drown, rocks can fall on you, you can fall on rocks. It happens all the time. Wear good shoes, not rubber slippers, and keep both your eyes and ears open. Flash floods do occur.

Theft

Theft can be a problem, though I don't believe it's that big a problem on Maui. In fact, crime in Hawaii is generally low and getting lower. Data that just came out stated that the crime rate in the islands is at its lowest level since they started collecting data in 1975. That said, it's still something I think about every time I walk away from my parked car. There are a couple of things I do that I believe keep me from becoming a statistic.

First, if when I get out of the car I see a lot of broken glass in the area, I consider that a very bad sign and move on. If the parking area seems safe enough, I get out and get going quickly by not fumbling around with my gear in the back seat or the trunk. Sometimes I will pull off the road to do that, organizing before I get to my destination. Of course, never leave anything valuable in sight. I know I should not say this (bad luck), but in over 30 years of do-

underestimate it. Don't think you will hear the wave coming. By the time you do it will be too late. Generally the surf is bigger on the North shore in the winter and the South shore in the summer, but that is not always the case. There can be long periods between swells. A few years ago, on the south shore of Kauai in the winter, I had been paddling along the coast for a couple of hours and had not seen any wave over 2 feet, so I was not looking out. Suddenly, a 6-foot-high wave came in and threw me up on the rocks. My kayak broke in half. All my gear, even the camera equipment in dry bags, was lost. Many people have been pulled off beaches or out of tide pools by waves they were not expecting. You should always watch out and, if you can, have someone watch you.

Keep Out!

ing this I have never had any of my camera gear stolen.

The Unwelcome Mat

KEEP OUT, STAY OUT, TABOO, and KAPU are some of the signs you are likely to see in restricted areas. They all mean the same thing, and you should pay attention to them, especially on Maui. A few very popular guidebooks have lately promised to reveal the hidden Maui. Unfortunately, much of the Maui they reveal is hidden on private property and the people who live there are becoming increasingly unhappy about uninvited visitors. These guidebooks also recommend some sites that are downright dangerous: people have had to be rescued from hikes in rough areas; others have drowned on remote shorelines with big waves.

The Ocean

The ocean is the most dangerous part of Maui. You should never take your eye off it and never

A roadside marker at Nahiku

I. The Hana Coast

General Description: Many people, including me, consider the Hana Coast the most beautiful section of Maui. It's only about 30 miles long, but it's full of streams, waterfalls, pools, beaches, gardens, and hikes. You could spend days here, and you really should spend at least one night in Hana.

Most people do it as a day trip though. It may only be 30 miles each way, but it's a long 30 miles. The road is not as bumpy as it used to be, but there are still over 600 curves and 50 bridges, and many of those are one lane. This chapter will cover from Paia town at the start of the Hana Road to Kipahulu and seven pools that are a few miles past Hana.

It's possible to keep driving the road around to Haleakala and Upcountry Maui and wind up back in Kahalui. That part of the road is even narrower and rougher, and it's often closed because of bad weather (you can call 808-986-1200 to check). It's an interesting drive, but it's not all that photogenic because it goes through a very dry area.

While it is possible to drive the Hana Coast counterclockwise, starting at Haleakala, I do not recommend it. You will probably get to Kipahulu sooner, but after that will be swimming upstream, with a couple thousand cars headed your way. I have only done it once. The timing for photography is not as good in this direction either.

You need to start on the east side, and you really should start early. I am usually driving past Paia before the sun comes up. This gets me to the dramatic cliff areas of the coast just when the sun is first striking them. I then usually stop several times before I reach the Ke'anae Peninsula. Ke'anae is about the halfway point. This is where I get caught by the

Where: The eastern slope and coastline of Haleakala
Noted For: Very beautiful drive, waterfalls, pools, gardens, flowers, rainforest, and hiking
Best Time: The earlier the better, and the road gets crowded by 9 A.M.
Peak Time: Any sunny day by noon
Facilities: At state parks and beaches along the way
Parking: At parks and some places along the road
Sleeps and Eats: There are only a couple of hotels at Hana Town and a few scattered B&Bs. There are some good road stands along the way for food, especially at Nahiku.
Sites Included: Twin Falls, Waikamoi Nature Trails, Garden of Eden, Lower Puohokamoa Falls, Ke'anae Arboretum, Ke'anae Peninsula, Wailua, Waikani Falls, Pua'a Ka'a State Park, Nahiku, Kahana Garden, Wai'anapanapa Park, Hana Town, Hamoa Beach, Wailua Falls, Kipahulu, Seven Pools, Kaupo

hordes of tourists in Jeeps and Mustangs that are on the road every day. Traffic moves more slowly from there on. It seems everybody is driving as if they are on vacation. You should slow down as well because from here to Kipahulu opportunities abound.

There are a few items you should take with you down the coast. The first one you might consider is a convertible (join the crowd, Mustangs are my favorite). Usually I am not a fan of convertibles, but on the Hana Coast they are a lot of fun, and they reduce fatigue and the potential for car sickness. You will also see a lot more. This actually helps your photography, and it may be worth renting one, even if just for one day. Bring some sunscreen, water, and food, especially if you leave early, because you won't find anything till you are about halfway along the coast. Once you get past Ke'anae there will be some good roadside stands to eat at, and there are a couple of restaurants and stores in Hana.

There will be plenty of photographic opportunities, rain or shine. Generally when it's sunny I gravitate toward the coastline and beaches of Kipahulu, Hamoa, or Wai'anapanapa. On the coastline the weather will change often and quickly, so with a little patience you can usually get what you need. When it's cloudy or rainy I move toward the mountains, streams, and waterfalls, either beside the road or on hikes. For this part of Maui I actually enjoy the cloudy days more. The rainforests and gardens photograph better in soft light. You definitely need a tripod, and a large umbrella is a good idea as well.

When I am doing the round-trip in one day it usually takes me twice as long to get to my turn-around spot as it does to drive out. However there are a couple of locations that might be better seen and photographed on the return trip, and I will point these out in the chapter.

Pro Tip: Take a tripod! When shooting coastlines in Hawaii I sometimes leave my tripod in the car, but I always have it on the Hana Coast.

Lower Twin Falls

You're going to see lots of streams and water-falls and a dense rainforest. The tripod is needed for controlling depth of field (range of focus). It will also give you the ability to use slow shutter speeds to get the flowing water effect on waterfalls and streams. For these it's necessary to get down to 1/4 or 1/2 second on the shutter speed.

Another item that will help is a polarizing filter. Many point-and-shoot digital cameras only go down to around F8. The polarizing filter will make it two stops darker and that will help you get to 1/4 second. You can also twist it to enhance the greens in the photo. Also, when trying to do flowing-water photos, set your ISO as low as possible.

Twin Falls (1)

Shortly past mile marker 2 you will see a fruit stand on the right-hand side of the road. This is the beginning of the trails back to the Twin Falls area, and it's the first waterfall opportunity on the Hana Coast. It's by no means the best, though, and you probably should skip it if you're trying to get down the coast early, or catch it on the way back. If you're late or you're not really going all the way down the coast it is a good area and a nice hike. There are a couple of falls up at the end of the hike, but there is also a lower one very close to the road.

Directions: It's just past mile marker 2 on the right. You can park on either side of the bridge and follow the stream a couple of hundred yards up to the lower falls.

Waikamoi Nature Trail (2)

The Waikamoi Trails are on the right-hand side between mile markers 9 and 10. There are two loops, one quite short and one that takes 30 to 45 minutes to walk. The trails are wide, well-maintained, and easy to walk, and you'll find a variety of plants and flowers and a few nice

Tropical flowers at Garden of Eden

overlooks. There are also some benches along the trails, so it's a good place to break for lunch.

Directions: Park on right side between mile markers 9 and 10.

Garden of Eden (3)

If the whole coast is like a botanical garden, why would you want to pay $10 to see a private one? This family-run garden is quite well done, and contains a wide variety of tropical plants. You can drive through it or walk it, but

Lower Puohokamoa Falls

it is fairly steep; I recommend driving to the top first. There you will get a stunning view down to the coast. If you walk to the side you can photograph Upper Puhokamoa Falls. About a third of the way back down on the right-hand side is a small building. In that area you will find tropical flowers, including gingers and heliconia. Most of them are labeled with common and Latin names. As with most gardens, here I tend to use my 24–105mm zoom or 100mm macro lens and a tripod.

Directions: At about mile marker 11 you will see the entrance to the Garden of Eden on the right.

Lower Puohokamoa Falls (4)

Drivers often miss Lower Puohokamoa Falls. There are no signs. From where you park there is a path that can get you to a very good view of the waterfall. Actually there are three views along the way, and the third is probably the best; it only takes about five minutes to reach. Be careful if it's wet and slippery, and don't go too far as the trail gets tough. Definitely take your tripod.

Directions: At about 3/4 of a mile past mile marker 10 is a turnout on the left-hand side that will hold about a half dozen cars.

DIVERSION: Guided Hikes

Is it better to take a guided hike or go on your own? It depends. I almost always go on my own, and that usually means by myself. I have a pace that is very erratic when I'm doing serious photography. I don't like to wait for people when I want to get somewhere while the light is right. People don't like to wait for me while I spend 20 minutes photographing a flower. That is the nature of nature photography.

Guided hikes can be a good choice though, and there are some excellent ones on Maui. Hike Maui is a tour company that has been in operation on Maui for over 25 years. Their guides are exceptionally well prepared and knowledgeable. Ken Schmitt, the owner, has explained the choice this way: "All trails on Maui are free or inexpensive. You should go on our tour only if you want to save yourself a lot of research, have a guide do the driving on difficult roads, be provided with complete outfitting and a fascinating narrative, have all your questions answered, and be well cared for by a competent, professional guide who will take a personal interest in you."

I tend to agree with that assessment. If you only want to photograph, or just get to a waterfall and swim, then a guide is a waste of time and money. However on a guided hike you will learn a lot more, have freedom from the pressure of how to get there, and if you're traveling with someone, your companion will have somebody else to talk to while you photograph. One idea might be to make your first hike guided, then go on your own.

Hike Maui
    www.hikemaui.com/story.html,
    866-324-6284
Maui Hiking Safaris
    www.mauihikingsafaris.com,
    888-445-3963

Ke'anae Arboretum (5)

Just before the turnoff to Ke'anae Peninsula you will see Ke'anae Arboretum on the right-hand side. It's a free state-run botanical garden where you'll see many ornamental, fruit, and timber tree species as well as around 150 varieties of tropical plants. (Not all are indige-

nous.) There are a couple of pleasant hikes here, though this is one place where, if you had someone to explain what you were seeing, it would be more enjoyable.

Directions: The arboretum is on the right side past mile marker 16.

Ke'anae Peninsula (6)

Ke'anae Peninsula is a place you could easily spend all day photographing. Shortly after the turn into the peninsula you will get a beautiful view across the taro fields of the peninsula. I have photographed this several times at various times of the day. From here you can shoot a panorama or use a telephoto lens to pick out interesting compositions.

A couple of hundred yards farther down the road you'll be at sea level and will see palm trees on the left. These are great to frame a photo of the coast and the Hana Road. There is also very jagged lava rock. If the surf is up, the waves crashing into these rocks can be spectacular here and on the other side of the peninsula. You can get in as close as is safe to shoot with a wide angle or stay back and work with a telephoto. If you have your tripod and polarizer, try some slow shutter photos. These will often give more of a feeling of motion and power. Experiment with exposures from 1/2 second to 1/15 second to see what works best. If you're lucky or dedicated enough to be here very early or very late, you can expand this to very long exposures to get some surreal effects of the lava and water.

The Ke'anae Congregational Church is well worth walking around and photographing. It was built in 1863 with lava rock walls. The church also has an interesting cemetery. Many of the headstones have photographs on them; you'll see this in a lot of Hawaiian cemeteries. I am not sure how these photos withstand decades in the tropical sun without fading.

Ke'anae Peninsula

This church is still actively in use by the community. Please be careful and respectful.

There is a rock and black sand beach at the end of the dirt road. You have to park about a mile away and walk in. At the end of the road, find the trail at the left that leads along the coastline to the beach. The rocks are hard to walk on, but in the middle is some black sand. Swimming is a bit dangerous but you can go in the freshwater pond behind the beach.

Aunty Sandy's Fruit Stand has good sandwiches and fantastic banana bread.

Directions: The turnoff is on the left between mile markers 16 and 17.

Pro Tip: Keʻanae is one of the places on Maui where I shoot a lot of panoramics. There are several ways to do this. The easiest is to just crop your photo. If you have a sharp lens and are not planning to print the photo up large, that is fine. Several point-and-shoot digital cameras have a program that will make a panorama for you, and some work well.

I used to have a couple of film cameras that were specifically for panoramas but now that I am 100 percent digital I mainly use the stitch method. This involves shooting several overlapping photos and stitching them together in postproduction. I use Photoshop, but there are other much less expensive programs that can do it. A few tips are to shoot verticals with about 30 percent overlap. I also use manual exposure and turn off the auto white balance. This keeps the exposure and color consistent between the frames.

This technique will work well for most pans. Where it is less effective is along the coastline when there are waves. The placement of waves will change from frame to frame and there is no way to line them up. Sometimes it's not that noticeable, but usually it is. Then the only digital option is to crop one photo into a panoramic.

Wailua (7)

Back on the road to Hana there will be a couple of overlooks on the left-hand side. One will be of Keʻanae Peninsula, and the other of Wailua. Both are worth a stop and, if the weather is good, both offer a good panoramic view of taro fields and the coast.

Shortly past mile marker 18 is the turnoff down to Wailua. I do not recommend it. The people of Wailua have become tired of tourists in rental cars. This will become evident to you by the number of KEEP OUT and KAPU signs you will see. There's even one that says, IF YOU DON'T LIVE HERE YOU DON'T BELONG HERE. I can't really blame them and might feel the same way if I lived there. Photographically you're not missing much anyway. There is no access to the shore, and much of what is here can be better photographed in Keʻanae (where they still want you).

Directions: Wailua is just past mile marker 18 on the right.

Waikani Falls (8)

Waikani Falls is shortly past the Wailua Overlook. There is very little parking here so grab a spot if you see one. You can shoot the falls from the Kahalui side of the bridge or you can do a short hike in from the Hana side. There are three strands (sometimes called

Waikani Falls

A waterfall at Puaʻa Kaʻa State Park

Three Bears) to this waterfall, which makes it more of a horizontal composition. This waterfall makes for a very nice slow exposure image.

Directions: Waikani Falls is past mile marker 19 on the right.

Puaʻa Kaʻa State Park (9)

Puaʻa Kaʻa is before mile maker 23. Lots of cars stop here, mainly for the restrooms. There are a couple of waterfalls right over the hill, though, that are easy to get to, photograph, and swim in.

If you're looking for something less crowded and more beautiful, you can do a fairly easy hike up to another waterfall from the right side of the lower waterfall. The trail starts out kind of steep then branches out, but all the branches lead up to an irrigation canal. From there you make a left across a bridge. The bridge has no railing, so if you're unsure or unsteady don't do it. At the end of the bridge is a trail to the right, and within 100 yards you'll see the waterfall. This is one of my favorites on the island. The best view is from the top. There is a very short side trail before you go down to the pond.

Directions: The parking and restrooms are on the left and the waterfalls are on the right between mile markers 22 and 23.

Kahanu Garden

Nahiku (10)

Nahiku is kind of a combination of Wailua and Ke'anae. It's not as dramatically beautiful as Ke'anae. While it's not as unfriendly as Wailua, there is still little access here. This makes it wonderful to drive through but difficult to photograph. Time would probably be better spent down the road at Wai'anapanapa.

Back on the main road toward Hana is the Nahiku Marketplace. Here they have a series of roadside stands with practically every ethnic food in Hawaii. It really is a good place to stop and eat.

Directions: Nahiku Road is just past the mile marker 25 on the left.

Kahanu Garden (11)

Good news! One of the best gardens in all Hawaii is down Ulaino Road at mile marker 31. It holds a large collection of native species, which are the plants Polynesians brought with them in outrigger sailing canoes. Pi'ilanihale Heiau is here also. It dates from the 1500s and is the largest Hawaiian temple site in the state.

Bad news! This garden is only open from 10 A.M. to 2 P.M., which is the worst time of day to photograph anything, but it's especially hard for plants and flowers. If it's cloudy, you might be able to get some good shots, and it's certainly worth seeing anyway.

At the end of this road is Blue Pool, which used to be a wonderful place to go to, but it had become overrun by tourists. The people who own the property you had to cross to get to it have closed it down.

Directions: Pass mile marker 31 and turn left on Ulaino Road. The entrance to the garden is about 1 1/2 miles down on the right-hand side.

Wai'anapanapa Park (12)

Wai'anapanapa, at mile marker 32, is a place where you really should stop and plan on spending some time. It has over 130 acres of some of the most beautiful coastline on Maui. Wai'anapanapa also has the best black sand beach on the island, as well as coastline hikes in either direction, a freshwater pool in a cave, campgrounds, and cabins. You can call 808-984-8109 for information on camping and cabins.

Photographically, Wai'anapanapa is best early or late. This is also when you'll find it least crowded. Personally I like the hike to the left. This is another area where it's good to shoot panoramas or long exposures.

Directions: Just beyond mile marker 32 is a sign to turn left into the park. Follow the narrow road all the way down and to the left. That is where the parking for the black sand beach is.

Hana Town (13)

You might think Hana is at the end of the Hana Road but it's not. The road goes on for quite a way, all the way around Halakaka if you stay on

it. Hana Town sits behind Hana Bay and is home to the Hana Cultural Center & Museum (small but interesting), and the Hana Hotel, as well as a few other places to stay. If you're spending a few days in Hana you are probably in this area. There are a few fishing boats working out of Hana Bay, and sometimes you can find outrigger canoes paddling in the afternoon. The afternoon is also a good time to hike up to the cross on the hill behind the town. There is a good view in all directions from there.

There is a unique beach in Hana. It's called

Black sand beach at Waiʻanapanapa Park

Kaihalulu but is better known as Red Sand Beach. It's on the back side of Hana Bay and is reached by a somewhat dangerous and slippery trail. The trail is off Uakea Road; once you pass the school, cut through the empty lot down to the coast and the trail goes off to the left. The last time I was there the trail was worse than ever, so if you go, be careful. Another caution is that when you get there you may find people who seem to have forgotten their swimsuits. You can decide if that is good or bad. However, be aware that nudity is officially illegal.

Directions: About a half mile past mile marker 33 the road splits. The upper road will take you down the coast to Kipahulu. The lower road goes to Hana Bay.

Koki Beach and Hamoa Beach (14)

A couple of miles farther up Hana Road are two more beaches, Koki and Hamoa. It's mainly surfers who use Koki Beach; the sand is kind of coarse for other purposes. There is a good view of Alau Island from here. This is a very good spot to shoot the sunrise or time-lapse coastline photos.

Right around the corner is Hamoa, which is the whitest beach on the Hana Coast. There is a good view of it from the top left side or you can hike down to photograph from either end.

Directions: Turn left on Haneo'o Road, which is about a mile past Hana. This is a loop road

Kaihalulu (Red Sand Beach)

Sunrise on Koki Beach

that will take you past both beaches and bring you back up to the Hana Road.

Wailua Falls (15)

The area past Hamoa Beach down to just past Oheʻo Gulch (Seven Pools) is generally considered to be Kipahulu. If you're doing the coast in one day, you'll probably be pretty tired by the time you get to Kipahulu. You will also have missed the best time of day in Kipahulu, which is the morning. There is a lot to see and do in Kipahulu, and it would be good to spend at least a day there. The mile markers switch directions on this side, and you'll be counting down instead of up.

The first place you will probably want to stop is Wailua Falls. When it has rained recently and there's enough water, it's one of the most beautiful falls in Hawaii. It's easy to photograph from the bridge and just a short walk

back to the pool. This spot gets very crowded, so you should try to arrive early.

Directions: Wailua Falls is past mile marker 45 on the right.

Kipahulu, Oheʻo Gulch (Seven Sacred Pools) (16)

This area used to be called Seven Sacred Pools, but there are more than seven and the sacred part was made up. Now the area is called Oheʻo Gulch, and is part of Haleakala National Park, and the park service controls it. Park at the lot past mile marker 42 and pay a per-car fee of $10. From there you can hike along the coast back to the bridge that spans Oheʻo Gulch and the bottom pools. One of the best places to photograph is from the bottom pool looking up to the bridge. There are also several view possibilities along the left side of

Lower falls and bridge at Kipahulu

the stream heading back up to the bridge. The spot where the stream goes into the ocean can be dramatic as well, but be cautious of waves and salt spray. Don't forget your tripod.

Directions: Go over the high bridge that spans Ohe'o Gulch. The parking is about a half mile farther on the left-hand side.

Caution: This is the turn-around place for most people trying to do the whole coast in one day. It can get very crowded from about noon to 3 P.M.; if you can avoid those hours, you'll have a better time. Also, if you're driving back late, be very alert. You and everybody else will be tired. You will probably be going very slowly, so a life-threatening accident is unlikely, but there are a lot of small accidents waiting to happen on the way back.

Pipiwai Trail (17)

This is my favorite hike on the island. It's about 4 miles round-trip and is moderately difficult, taking two to four hours. The trail follows the stream up past several pools and waterfalls. Makahiku Waterfall is about 200 feet high. There are several trails to explore. You can find several pools to photograph or swim in.

Be careful though: a friend of mine and I jumped into one of the pools from about 10 feet up. We did not scout the situation well enough beforehand and found no place to climb back up before the pool went over a waterfall. It took about 15 minutes of one of us pushing the other up so he could get a handhold to pull us both out. It was funny at the time but would not have been if water started to come up and push us over the waterfall.

Farther up there is a bamboo forest. I advise staying on the trail here because I got lost in that bamboo forest for about an hour. At the top of the trail you'll find the 400-foot Waimoku Falls. The trail comes out so close to the falls that it's difficult to photograph without a very wide-angle lens.

Directions: Use the same parking lot as Ohe'o Gulch. The trailhead is back toward the gulch.

Kaupo (18)

Most cars go back the way they came along the Hana Coast. When I drive the coast in one day, I start at first light and when I leave the Seven Pools area, I keep going around through Kaupo. The road is rough but usually you do not need a four-wheel-drive vehicle to do it. Once you leave the Kipahulu area the climate and scenery change quickly. It will probably be hot, dry, and windy. The only place I stop is Kaupo, where you'll find the Kaupo Store and my favorite church site in Hawaii. Huialoha Church was built in 1859. Carl Lindquist and other members of the Hana community recently restored the church. Its stark white façade stands out against the dramatic coastline on this lonely stretch of shoreline.

Directions: To get to the church look for a dirt road on the ocean side about 3/10 of a mile past mile marker 36. It may be chained but not locked. The last time I was there, the road was barely passable with a regular car, so you may want to walk. You will have to go about 1/4 of a mile down before you see the church. The Kaupo Store is farther up the road near mile marker 35.

Huialoha Church in Kaupo

A view of the West Maui Mountains by helicopter

II. Central Maui

General Description: Central Maui is generally considered to be the relatively flat area between Haleakala and the West Maui Mountains. It's the commercial hub of the island and includes Kahalui, Wailuku, and the airport. It's here that you'll find the county government, Maui Community College, and large stores such as Costco and Walmart. There is a photo shop in the strip mall just across from KMart.

It's not the most scenic part of the island, with the exception of Iao Valley, which is beautiful in any weather. Wailuku town is interesting, and the beaches of Kanaha and Hookipa are alive with world-class windsurfing and kiteboarding.

Wailuku (19)

Wailuku is the capital of Maui County. It's an old town and has that feeling. It missed the development that other areas of the island have seen. Up at the top of Ka'ahumanu Street (Main Street) you will find the old New England-style Ka'ahumanu Church. It was built in 1876. The Bailey House Museum is there also. They do not allow photography but do have an interesting collection of Hawaiian artifacts collected by the missionary Edward Bailey.

The most interesting place to photograph is probably Market Street, which cuts across Main Street. It's here that you'll find unique shops, restaurants, and galleries, as well as the historic Iao Theater. They are all housed in old plantation-style buildings.

Directions: Wailuku is nestled above Kahalui and below Iao Valley. Drive up Ka'ahumanu Avenue, which turns into Main Street after the stone bridge.

Where: The flat area between Haleakala and West Maui Mountains from Wailuku to Paia to Ma'alea Harbor

Noted For: It is the residential and commercial heart of the island. The wind howls through the gap between the two mountains, so windsurfers and kiteboarders love it.

Best Times: Morning for Wailuku and Iao Valley, and afternoon for the beaches

Facilities: At Iao Valley State Park, Kanaha Beach Park, and Hookipa Beach Park

Parking: At parks or gardens

Sleeps and Eats: There are only a couple of hotels in Kahalui. They are not great, but they are cheap (for Maui). There is no shortage of restaurants though. You'll find all the chains in Kahalui. For something more interesting I would suggest going to Café O'Lei, Saengs Thai, or Tasty Crust (breakfast) in Wailuku. In Paia I like Café Mambo, Paia Fish Market, and the Flatbread Company for pizza. Mama's Fish House just outside of Paia is also excellent but a bit overpriced.

Sites Included: Wailuku, Iao Valley, Kahalui, Kanaha Beach Park, Paia, Hookipa Beach Park, Kanaha Pond and Bird Sanctuary, Kealia Natural Wildlife Refuge, Ma'alaea Harbor, McGregor Point, Molokini Island

Pro Tip: If you're on Maui during the first Friday of any month there is a First Friday celebration on Market Street in Wailuku. The celebration starts at 5 P.M., and the street is lined with booths selling arts, crafts and food. There is music and usually a hula halau or two will dance.

Whenever you are on Maui, there is probably a celebration somewhere. So, if you're interested, you should check the newspapers, the

Internet, or with your hotel desk to see what is happening.

When I go to something like this I try to show up a little early. If it's a parade I will go to the staging area. At these times people are usually happy to be photographed, and this is when I shoot portraits. Once the event or parade starts, they are busy. It's harder to work with them, so this is when I shoot the activity. In the staging area or during the prep for an event I will ask for permission before I photograph someone. This can be as simple as holding up your camera and getting a nod from them before you start. Most people in Maui are happy to do it, but not everybody, so I try to tread lightly.

Iao Valley (20)

Iao Valley is a couple of miles straight up from the top of Wailuku. It was formed as the center of a large volcanic crater. What was once black and red is now solid green. At the end of the road are several trails and loops that are easy to hike. From these you can photograph the stream, some small falls, and Iao Needle. Iao Needle is the tall spire on the right-hand side

First Friday celebration in Wailuku

just as you go in. It's usually photographed from the bridge. I prefer to walk down to the stream and include the bridge in the composition or do a slow shutter shot of the steam and needle.

Between the Iao Needle and Wailuku are a few other spots of interest: Hawaii Nature Center, Kepaniwai Heritage Gardens, and Maui Tropical Gardens. Hawaii Nature Center has some displays that are especially good for children. Kepaniwai Heritage Gardens are free and showcase the diversity of Maui, with sections representing Hawaiian, Japanese, Portuguese, Filipino, and Caucasian cultures.

My favorite of these though is Maui Tropical Gardens. It's a medium-sized garden that is just packed with all kinds of tropical plants and flowers. It's well maintained and easy to get around. Being back up against the mountain, it is quite often overcast up here. That is exactly what I want when photographing a botanical garden. When I was doing my *Pua Nani, Gardens of Hawaii* book, I would show up on rainy days and would be told, "You should have been here yesterday, it was sunny." Very few photos in that book were shot on sunny days. For gardens I like to have clouds, maybe a little rain, a tripod, and, of course, mosquito repellent. I don't like sun and I hate wind.

Directions: If you take Main Street up through Wailuku, and keep going straight, you will go up into Iao Valley State Park.

Kahalui (21)

There is not much to photograph in Kahalui. It is a residential area with lots of shopping and light industry around the edges. You can get your supplies here. Costco has some photo equipment if you need an extra card. There is a beach in the harbor right behind the Maui Seaside Hotel. There may be some outrigger canoe activity there in the late afternoon.

The Alexander and Baldwin Sugar Museum

Directions: When you get off the plane you are in Kahalui. The town and shopping centers are mostly along Ka'ahumanu Avenue.

DIVERSION: The Alexander and Baldwin Sugar Museum

The Alexander and Baldwin Sugar Museum is in the plantation town of Puunene. This is right in the center of Maui. On most days you can see smoke coming out of the stacks of the mill. While this used to be a common sight in the islands, the Puunene Mill is now the last one operating in Hawaii.

A fruit stand at a farmers' market

The museum is next to the mill and has both interior and exterior displays. On the exterior you can see and photograph old tractors and diggers as well as an 1880s steam locomotive.

The 1,800-square-foot interior of the museum has several rooms that cover the history of sugar in Maui, the field workers, and the mill operations. There are great displays with old photographs and murals throughout.

> Admission is $7.00 for adults, $5.00 for seniors (65 and older), and $2.00 for children (6–12). Children under 6 are free.
> Mon.–Sat., 9:30 A.M. to 4:30 P.M.;
>   808-871-8058
> 3957 Hansen Rd., Puunene

DIVERSION: Farmers' Markets

Most every day there is a farmers' market somewhere on Maui. They move around a lot so the information here may be incorrect before this book is even printed. However markets can be a great place to photograph people, produce, and flowers as well as a good spot to pick up picnic supplies.

The Green Dragon Farmers Market is held at the Kahalui Shopping Center 7 A.M. to 4 P.M. Tuesday, Wednesday, and Friday. They are also at the Kukui Mall in Kihei, same hours Tuesday through Friday. On Saturday you can go to the Maui Swap Meet across from the Kahalui Post Office from 6 A.M. to 1 P.M. In Hana, Ono Organic Farms operates across from the Hasegawa Store Sunday through Thursday, 10:30 A.M. to 4: P.M.

If you do not want to chase around, there are two stores called "Farmers Market." One is in Kihei at 61 S. Kihei Rd. just across from Sugar Beach and the other between Kaanapali and Napili at 3636 Lower Honoapiilani Rd. They both have all the local organic fruits, vegetables, juices, flowers, and breads that you would expect.

Kanaha Beach Park (22)

Kanaha Beach is the hub of windsurfing and kiteboarding activity on Maui. The sailing may be more extreme or dramatic farther up the coast at Hookipa, but at Kanaha there are more sailors and some of the action is very close. There is also outrigger canoe paddling right offshore on most afternoons.

You'll find the windsurfers off to the right and the kiteboarders all the way to the left around the corner, in an area called Kite Beach. You can see them so it's not hard to find.

Generally I find windsurfing easier to photograph than kiteboarding. The sailor, the board, and the sail are all together, and it's just a matter of lining it up with a background and using the biggest telephoto lens I have with me.

Kanaha Beach Park

Kite Beach in Kanaha

Kiteboarding is a bit more difficult. The distance of the kite from the rider makes it hard to get both in any effective composition with a telephoto. My favorite shot at Kite Beach is to stand right at the edge of the water where the kiteboarders launch. That is where they come in and do a speed jibe or jump, and you can get the rider close to you with the kite above and the West Maui Mountains behind. It is best in the afternoon when the better kiteboarders show up.

Pro Tip: Kanaha is a good place to try some pan-motion photos. Experiment with slowing your shutter speed down to 1/8, 1/15, or 1/30 of a second, framing the sailor and panning with the sailor as you release the shutter.

One of the great things about digital photography is that you can immediately see what you've got and make adjustments. What you are trying to get is flowing water that gives the impression of speed while keeping as much as possible of the windsurfer sharp. This does not work as well with kiteboarders because they move up and down too much. It will work much better if you have a fluid pan on your tripod, but if you have steady hands it can be done hand-held. I find that when I use a tripod I like one in five photos; hand-held drops the number I like down to maybe one in 10. Of course, another great thing about digital is that taking a lot of photographs costs nothing but time.

Directions: Kanaha Beach Park can be a little tricky to get to. It's adjacent to the airport, and one route is to drive all the way through the airport and make a right on Hemaloa Street where the car rentals are. This will bring you to the middle of Kanaha Beach Park. For the other way take Hana Highway (HI 36) into Kahalui and veer off to the right on HI 361. Turn right on Amala Place, which runs along the shore till it ends at Kanaha Beach.

Helicopter Tours (23)

Helicopter tours are a fantastic (and expensive) way to see and photograph Maui. They all operate out of the back of the Kahalui Airport and offer several different tours. My favorite is to head over to the North Shore of Molokai, which is spectacular. It has some of the highest sea cliffs and waterfalls in the world, and you get to see the West Maui Mountains on the way. Another good trip includes the Hana Coast, Upcountry Maui, and Haleakala. This trip will take you through several different climate zones.

Directions: All helicopter tours operate out of the Kahalui Airport. The helipads are on the opposite side of the runways from the main terminal. There is an access road that goes around counterclockwise.

Pro Tip: I have shot a number of aerial books on the islands, including one on Maui. I used to shoot all medium-format transparencies, but the digital world has surpassed that level of quality. Right now I use a Canon 5D Mark II with 16–35mm and 24–105mm lenses. I set a low ISO, usually 100, and shutter speed of 1/500 of a second or faster.

Most of my aerial work is done on a chartered helicopter, so we take the door off. If I have to shoot through a window, I try to wear a large, long-sleeved black shirt. Sometimes I will pull the sleeves over my hands. This is all to try to cut down on reflections. I also try to get the camera as close to the glass as I can without touching it. If you touch the glass, there will be way too much vibration, plus if it's plastic you risk scratching it.

Paia (24)

If you're driving the Hana Coast, you will probably pass through Paia too early to see much, or photograph anything. If you have slept in a little, though, it is a good place to get provisions and maybe take a few photos of the town. It's kind of a funky old sugar mill town with a main street of brightly painted two-story wooden buildings that now house a number of great shops, galleries, and restaurants.

If you are doing the round-trip to Hana, Paia is the first place that you pass. I suggest you make it an afternoon stop. The town itself is probably best photographed late in the day from the ocean side of the street. I know that seems wrong, like you will be on the east side shooting into the sun. That is not the case. The sweep of the island turns things around. If you look at a map you can see what I mean.

You can walk the whole town in about 15 minutes. What I often do in Paia and other small towns is just grab one camera and one wide to telephoto lens (mine is 24mm–105mm). With that I can shoot architectural wide shots or details of the place. Paia is a colorful place, not just the buildings but also the

A view of the Hana Coast by helicopter

people. Here you'll find windsurfers, kite-boarders, surfers, artists, new age hippies, and bikers (both kinds).

Directions: Paia is the first town on the Hana Road, which is also called HI 36 here, at mile marker 6.

DIVERSION: Shopping

Paia has a number of unique stores, all kinds of restaurants, and some of Maui's best art galleries. It's a great place to end a Hana trip or a day in Central Maui. A couple of my favorite relatively inexpensive places to eat are Café Mambo and Paia Fish Market. If you want to take your time, Mama's Fish House is good, has a great setting, but is much more expensive. Mama's is about a mile out on the Hana side of town.

Hookipa Beach Park (25)

Hookipa is one of the most famous spots in world for windsurfing and kiteboarding. The surf may be bigger down the road at Jaws, but you can only ride the waves at Jaws a few days a year. There will be sailors out at Hookipa on any windy day. Generally the wind here does not come up till about 10 A.M. and it dies after 3 P.M. This is because of a Venturi Effect, in which the heat of the day sucks the wind through the gap of Central Maui. On any normal trade wind day it will be blowing hard at Hookipa.

Hookipa is a great place to use your telephoto lenses. You can get right down on the beach, where the lens will make the waves stack up and look larger, or you can go up on the hill. There you'll have a better view of all that is happening, but you may need a longer lens.

If you have a waterproof housing or waterproof camera you can go out in the surf. I don't recommend it. I have done it a couple times, and it's the spookiest water photography expe-

Windsurfing at Hookipa Beach Park

rience I have had. The current is moving all over the place, so you better know how to swim very well. The real problem, though, is keeping an eye on everything. When photographing surfing you have to watch the waves and the surfers coming at you. Windsurfing and kiteboarding add a third dimension. They are also coming at you from behind, jumping waves, going up to 30 feet in the air, and landing who knows where. After a couple of close calls I decided to just shoot from the beach.

Directions: At mile marker 8, Hookipa Beach Park has a one-way road going through it so don't take the first turnoff from Hana Highway. If you go a little farther you'll see a sign for Hookipa. Turn left there and left again to drive down to the beach and parking.

Kanaha Pond and Bird Sanctuary (26)

The Kanaha Pond and Bird Sanctuary does not look like much from the outside but it's an important refuge for rare Hawaiian birds. You will see the black-necked stilt (ae'o), as well as the Hawaiian coot (alae) and Hawaiian duck (kaloa). It's a short walk to the observation

Golden Plover, Kolea, Kanaha Pond

area. Bring your telephoto, tripod, and binoculars if you have them.

Directions: The sanctuary is on Amala Road, as is Kanaha Beach Park. It's free.

Kealia Pond and Wildlife Refuge (27)

Kealia Pond and Wildlife Refuge is on the other shoreline of Central Maui, over by Ma'alaea Harbor. It's much larger than Kahana Refuge, 690 acres, and is home to 30 species of birds. The name *Kealia* means salt-encrusted place, and it was once a Hawaiian fishpond. There is a boardwalk that goes along the marsh area. Opportunities for photographing birds are excellent here.

Directions: If you go south on HI 310 from Ma'alaea toward Kihei there is an entrance to a gravel parking area between mile markers 1 and 2.

DIVERSION: Maui Ocean Center

Want to get some great underwater photos without having to get wet? Maui Ocean Center is your place. It's the best aquarium in Hawaii. There are numerous displays, exhibits, and activities. The highlight though is the 750,000 Open Ocean Exhibit, with an acrylic tunnel running through it. When you walk through this tube, you can photograph marine life in every direction.

    Location: At Ma'alaea Harbor
    www.mauioceancenter.com; 808-270-7000

McGregor Point (28)

McGregor Point can be a popular spot between November and May. That's because this is the easiest place to spot humpback whales on Maui during their season. It is also a lot cheaper than going out on a cruise, however you are not going to get spectacular whale pho-

Molokini Island

tos from here. On clear days it does have a good view of the expanse of Haleakala though. Early morning before the wind picks up and late afternoon are the best times.

Directions: The point and parking lot are on Honoapiilani Highway (HI 30) near mile marker 8.

Molokini Island (29)

Molokini Island is the rim of a partially sunken crater. It is about 2.5 miles offshore and has been made into an underwater sanctuary for marine life. If you're taking a tour out there

you'll probably be leaving from Ma'alaea Harbor. It's advisable to take the morning trip because the afternoon ones, while less expensive, can be rough and windy. The snorkeling is good out there, and if you have underwater camera gear you will use it here. From December through April you'll probably see whales as well. Good luck with whale photos though. It's probably the most frustrating photography I have ever done. They pop up all over the place, and I was always just a little too late. Actually it is not too hard to get shots of whales' tails, but catching the breaching out of the water takes lots of patience and luck.

A jacaranda tree in Haleakala

III. Haleakala and Upcountry

General Description: Upcountry Maui generally refers to the slopes of Haleakala, which are above Central Maui. It stretches from Haiku on the east side to Ulupalakua on the west. At the top is Haleakala National Park. Upcountry is known for gentle green slopes and curving country roads. There is a lot of farming up here, and you'll see diversified agriculture by every small road. There are numerous flower farms on the slopes of Haleakala with stunning orchids and protea.

When you drive up to Haleakala the landscape changes dramatically. At about 8,000 feet you rise above the tree line. The road curves many times as you drive to the 10,023-foot summit. There the views of the craters, West Maui, and the island of Hawaii are spectacular. Many people drive up for sunrise, however sunset can be just as inspiring. It's a good idea to plan on spending at least a day traveling around Haleakala and Upcountry.

Haiku (30)

Haiku is both a town and an area on the northeast side of Upcountry Maui. The town is on Haiku Road up from Hana Highway. Here

---

Where: The eastern slopes of Haleakala up to the summit. Haleakala Highway (HI 37) is the main road up, though there are numerous small, scenic roads up from Hana Highway.

Noted For: Beautiful green landscapes of Haiku, Makawao, and Kula, flower farms and gardens, country roads, and the drama of Haleakala Crater

Best Times: Morning is best on the east side, including the Haiku and Kokomo areas, then work your way around through Kula to Ulupalakua in the afternoon. On normal trade wind days it's common for clouds to build up on the east side in the morning and work their way around. Usually they stop somewhere around Kula.

Haleakala is really good at any time. However it's best early or late. A lot of people make the pilgrimage for sunrise every morning. Be aware that it's very cold up there at sunrise and the drive can be slow.

Facilities: Haleakala has all the facilities you would expect of a national park. Other than that it will be what you can find at restaurants, shops, and gardens.

Parking: Parking is not a problem anywhere.

Sleeps and Eats: The Kula Lodge and Kula Sandalwoods are about the only two hotel-type lodgings, however there are probably over 100 B&Bs in the area. Food is found mainly in the towns of Makawao, Haiku, Pukalani, and Keokea. Honestly, they grow the food up here but there are not that many good places to eat. A few exceptions are Grandma's Coffee in Keokea for breakfast or lunch, Makawao Steak House for dinner, and the Hana Hou Café in Haiku.

Another place that certainly deserves mention is the Haliimaile General Store, which is not a store at all. It's an excellent restaurant that features contemporary Hawaiian and Pacific Rim cuisine. It's at the bottom of Upcountry Maui, kind of out of the way at 900 Haili'imaile Road (HI 371). It's a wonderful place to stop for lunch or at the end of your day.

Sites Included: Haiku, Makawao, Kula, Kula Botanical Garden, Haleakala National Park, Poli Poli, Ulupalakua

---

you'll find most of the restaurants and stores. Photographically it's the area that is interesting. It includes Kokomo, Ulumau, and Kui'aha. There are several roads through the area and all go though verdant farmland. There is really no specific site to see here, it's about all the little things like painted mailboxes, fences made out of old windsurf boards, fields of flowers, and tree tunnels. It's probably best to see and photograph Haiku in the early morning. On many days here it will cloud up by 10 A.M., though soft light is still good for a lot of the close-up photo opportunities you'll find here.

Directions: From Upcountry Maui take Makawao Avenue (HI 40) across to Makawao and keep going straight. It will turn into Kapakalua Road (HI 365). You can follow that all the way to Hana Highway or cut off left or right on side roads to explore.

From Hana Highway go about a mile past Hookipa and you will see the right turn on Haiku Road. You can go up that or any of the next three roads to the right.

Makawao (31)

Makawao is the *paniolo* (Hawaiian for *cowboy*) town of Maui. Except for all the cars, it looks like it could be out of the Old West. Baldwin Avenue is full of small shops and art galleries. There are some good restaurants, like Makawao Steak House and Casanova's. You could go in the Komoda Store for great bakery goods and picnic supplies. While nearby Pukalani is actually a larger town, Makawao is much more interesting to shop in and see. Photographically it's a bit difficult because of all the cars. I prefer to shoot it late in the day and just wander up and down the main street.

Directions: From Haleakala Highway take Makawao Avenue (HI 40) over and that will bring you to the top of the town. From Hana

Makawao

Highway take Baldwin Avenue up from the center of Paia. It will bring you right up through the center of town.

Olinda Road (32)

This is my favorite drive in Upcountry Maui. It starts right above Makawao and goes straight up on a narrow road through beautiful rolling hills; when you get almost to the top you can turn left and come down equally scenic Piiholo Road. What you'll see up here is a mixture of farmland and private estates, many of which have been in families for generations.

Directions: Olinda Road starts right at the top of Makawao. If you take Baldwin Avenue straight up it turns into Olinda Road. If you take Piiholo Road back down it will end at Makawao Avenue very close to where you started.

Haleakala National Park (33)

Haleakala, at 10,023 feet, is the highest elevation on Maui. The road to the top was built in the 1930s, and it became part of the national park system. The park begins at about 7,500 feet. By 8,000 feet you are above the tree line. The winding road goes up to the summit with a couple of overlooks along the way.

There is a steady stream of cars going up early every day to see the sunrise. It can be a slow drive and very cold when you arrive, especially if it's windy. It is spectacular though. If there are any clouds you're almost always above them. Most people will drive all the way to the top. However a better view and photographic vantage point is from the Kalahaku Lookout at about 9,325 feet. Here you're looking across the calderas and cones in the crater and through a gap where you can see the island of Hawaii in the distance. I would recommend going to Kalahaku Lookout first and then up to the top.

Farmland off Olinda Road

Caution: I can't overstate how cold it can be up there before sunrise. Dress warmly and bring blankets. Plan on getting there at least 30 minutes before sunrise; the trip will take two to three hours from your hotel. You can call 1-866-944-5025 to get a weather forecast. If the forecast says it's going to be windy, you might want to skip sunrise.

Sunrise in Haleakala

At the summit you can see the whole expanse of Haleakala Crater. It's easy to see why this terrain was used to practice for moon landings. Haleakala means House of the Sun, and the sun beats down on this place relentlessly. Very little rain makes for a dry, barren landscape of red volcanic remains.

There are two trails from the summit, Sliding Sands Trail and Halemau Trail. Be aware though that both of these trails descend steeply, and it is not easy hiking back up at 10,000 feet. It's worth hiking down Sliding Sands at least partway, though. The view from inside looking up and out is really quite different, and you get a better appreciation of just how large Haleakala is.

There is a horseback touring company, Pony Express Tours, that does a ride all the way down to the floor of the crater. They can be reached at 808-667-2200 or www.pony expresstours.com. There are also several bike touring companies that offer rides down Haleakala. It is great fun but you can't carry a camera.

There is another stop farther down Haleakala at about 8,800 feet called Leleiwi Overlook. Most people go right by this one because you can't see the crater from the road or parking lot. It's about a five-minute hike from the lot to see the crater, but the view from here may be the best.

See the Specter of Brocken! It sounds like a roadside attraction but it's actually a natural phenomenon. If you stand on the crater rim with the sun behind you and clouds below, you'll see your own shadow on the cloud in the center of a circular rainbow. Native Hawaiians called it Ho'okuaka and considered it a view into the soul. At sunset, Leleiwi Lookout is one place you can do this.

Another thing to see on Haleakala is the silversword plant. The silversword is only found on Haleakala. The plant can live for 50 years. However, it is very delicate. Just walking around it can crush its roots and kill the plant, so when photographing it please keep a distance of at least 6 feet. These plants are rare, endangered, and protected; you risk fines if you disturb them. When the silversword blooms, it can be over 6 feet tall. After it blooms, it dies.

On your way out (or in) you may want to stop at Hosmer Grove. It's right inside the entrance to the park and has several hiking trails. At the beginning of the last century, Ralph Hosmer, Hawaii's first forester, brought in several types of trees hoping to start a timber industry. He planted pine, cedar, spruce, and eucalyptus. Only the pine and eucalyptus

Haleakala Crater from the top overlook

thrived. There are a few native species that grow in the grove as well. If you look you can see the hinahina (silver geranium) along the trail. There are signs along the way to explain what you're seeing. It's about a 30-minute hike.

In several spots on Haleakala you're likely to see the state bird, the nene. If it looks familiar, that's because it's a very close cousin of the Canada goose. These birds were hunted to the edge of extinction but are now protected.

DIVERSION: Haleakala Bike Tour

If you go up to Haleakala in the late morning you're certain to see streams of bikes coming back down. These are tours that start at the summit and ride all the way down, about 25 miles. It looks like fun and it certainly is. Is it safe? Well sort of, or maybe not really. In 2007 there were several accidents and three fatalities. The park service shut down all biking tours. The tours have started again but they no longer zip down the road from the top. They now start at the 6,500-foot level just outside the park. It's still an adventure, and a beautiful and exhilarating ride. There are about a half-dozen companies that offer various ride and tour packages. A couple of them go all the way to sea level. Haleakala Bike Company (808-575-9575, www.bikemaui.com) offers bikes that you can rent and take out on your own. While the changes have made this tour safer, there are still accidents quite often. If you're unsure of your abilities, this may not be a good choice.

The silversword plant, found only on Haleakala

Flower farm in Kula

Kula (34)

Kula is a section of Upcountry Maui that stretches from the turn off the road up to Haleakala all the way over to Keokea. It's the heart of the diversified agricultural movement in Hawaii, which started with the famous Maui onions. Now you'll find all kinds of exotic produce including coffee and protea at Shim Farm (625 Middle Rd., www.shimfarmtour.com), lavender at Alii Kula Lavender (1100 Waipoli Rd., www.aliikulalavender.com), and goat cheese at Surfing Goat Dairy (3651 Omaopio Rd., www.surfinggoatdairy.com). All three offer informal tours.

This area is famous for flowers as well, especially protea. One easy spot to see these is Sunrise Country Market on the way up to Haleakala. There is an excellent small protea garden to stroll through right in back of the market. It's also a good stop for supplies—food, flowers, or coffee.

An interesting site in Kula is the Holy Ghost Catholic Church, also known as the Octagon Church. It was built in the 1890s by Portuguese sugar plantation workers. It was recently restored and is beautiful both inside and out. The church is at 4300 Lower Kula Rd.

As with the areas around Makawao and Haiku, there are many small side roads worth checking out. A number of these connect HI 37 and HI 377. The roads going up from HI 377 are dead ends but are still worth seeing.

Directions: When you come up Haleakala Highway it will split just above Pukalani.

Catholic Holy Ghost Church, also known as the Octagon Church

Haleakala Highway (HI 377) on the left will take you to Haleakala, Kula Highway (HI 37) goes to the right. Both cut through the heart of Kula and join back together near Keokea, so it's a good idea to go out on one and back on the other.

Kula Botanical Garden (35)

Kula Botanical Garden is one of my favorite places in Maui and one of the best botanical gardens in Hawaii. It was started in 1968 and is really not that large. It only covers 8 acres. It's well laid out, though, and holds hundreds of varieties of unique plants as well as an excellent collection of protea and orchids. There are lots of close-up photographic opportunities here so bring a telephoto lens, macro lens, and a tripod.

Directions: Kula Botanical Garden is off HI 377 between Waiakoa Road and Alae Road.

Pro Tip: Kula Botanical Garden is one place I prefer to shoot when it's overcast. I know I will mainly be shooting close-ups there and these are much more colorful with soft light. Actually, whenever I go out in Maui I have a plan for what I will do if it's sunny and what I will do if it's cloudy. Gardens are often the choice when it's overcast. On Maui weather can change quickly. This is especially true on the slopes of Haleakala. It's always good to have a plan B.

Poli Poli (36)

Poli Poli (it's official name is Waipoli Road) is another road that goes high up onto the slopes of Haleakala. It does not make it to the summit and is not as scenic as the Haleakala Highway. If you are only up here one day it's doubtful you would have time to get to the top of Haleakala, see Kula, Makawao, and Haiku and still have time to drive up Waipoli Road. The upper portion may only be passable with four-wheel drive anyway.

Poli Poli would be worth it, though, if you're here for a couple days. There are some wonderful views across West Maui and toward Molokai and Lanai. At the top is Poli Poli State Park, with a redwood forest and a good hike through redwoods. It can also be a spectacular place to see and photograph the sunset.

If you go up Waipoli Road, you'll pass Alii Kula Lavender. If you love lavender you have found your place. Here they grow many varieties and use it in everything you can think of, and some things you've never thought of. The gardens around the main shop are photogenic as well.

Ulupalakua (37)

Ulupalakua is at the far southwest edge of Upcountry Maui. It's a wide-open area of farmland and ranches. From here you look down at Wailea and Makena and across the blue ocean to Kaho'olawe and Lanai. Here Kula Highway turns into Pi'ilani Highway and you can follow it all the way around to the Hana Coast. Pi'ilani Highway is actually a narrow, winding, scenic road, at least till it gets to Tedeschi Vineyards. After that it straightens out and goes through miles of dry, desolate country.

Tedeschi Vineyards is the turnaround spot for most people touring Upcountry Maui in one day. They have a tasting room and some nice grounds and gardens. They do offer tours three times a day, but there is really not that much to see or photograph during them. The actual vineyards are back toward Keokea.

The nearby Ulupalakua Ranch Store and

Kula Botanical Garden

Grill has some interesting local items, and hot food from 11 A.M. to 2:30 P.M. Ulupalakua Ranch has been around since 1845. It now covers 2,000 acres and holds about 6,000 head of cattle. Pardee Erdman now owns the ranch, and he has been working to keep the Hawaiian paniolo traditions going while protecting the native flora on ranch lands.

Directions: Take Kula Highway (HI 37) all the way out and it turns into Ulupalakua Road shortly past Keokea. This is the only road.

Tedeschi Vineyards in Ulupalakua

Ulupalakua

Kamaole Beach Park 2

IV. South Maui

General Description: South Maui is really Southwest Maui. It covers the area from Ma'alaea Harbor to La Perouse Bay. In between are some of the best beaches of Maui, Hawaii, and really the world. The shoreline goes through Kihei, Kamaole, Wailea, Makena, and the Ahihi-Kinau Natural Area Reserve. Most of the photographic opportunities are along the beaches.

If you look at the Google Earth satellite view of this shoreline, it really looks like one long beach with a few breaks of rocky points. The water can be a bit murky on the Ma'alaea end, but it gets much more clear as you move down the coast. From Kamaole to La Perouse Bay snorkeling is excellent.

When I photograph this coast I usually start early at the La Perouse end of the shoreline. This accomplishes two things. It avoids the crowds, and it's generally better lighting. The area beyond Makena can get very packed with cars by 10 A.M. I like to get out of there by then and maybe come back late in the day. There is also a line of clouds that forms in the morning almost every day that the trade winds are blowing. It comes off Haleakala and stretches out toward Kaho'olawe. It generally reaches farther out as the day heats up, then fades late in the

Where: This is the shoreline from Ma'alaea Harbor to La Perouse Bay. It starts as North Kihei Road, which merges into South Kihei Road. At Wailea the road turns uphill for a block. Turn right on Wailea Alanui Drive. This will become Makena Drive and will take you all the way to the end of the road.

Noted For: Beaches, golf courses, snorkeling, diving, kayaking, windsurfing, kiteboarding, resorts, and more beaches

Best Times: The first three hours and the last three hours of every day are best for beach photography. If you photograph too early or late, though, you will often miss the intense blue hues of the ocean here.

Facilities: Most of the beach parks have facilities that will be noted in the descriptions.

Parking: This is the one area on Maui where you may have a problem parking your car, especially if you show up late. The beach parks all have parking, but they are overwhelmed during the day. Down at Makena you will see cars parked on the road a half-mile from the beach. You should always be able to find something, except maybe in Wailea. Be prepared to walk. The good news is that it's all free.

Sleeps and Eats: There are way too many to name. Kihei Road is lined with condos, hotels, restaurants, and shops. A lot of visitors come and stay a month at a time. The more upscale resorts are in Wailea and Makena. Restaurants run the gamut from every chain you can think of to Spago or Mala. One place I am happy to recommend is Monsoon India at 760 S. Kihei Rd. It has great food, is right on the water, and has reasonable prices, which can be hard to find on Maui.

Sites Included: La Perouse Bay, Ahihi Cove, Pa'ako Beach, Makena Beach, Little Beach, Oneuli Beach, Malu'aka Beach, Po'olenalena Beach, Palauea Beach, Polo Beach, Wailea Beach, Mokapu Beach, Keawakapu Beach, Kamaole Beaches 1, 2, and 3, Hawaiian Islands Humpback Whale National Marine Sanctuary, Sugar Beach, Kealia Natural Wildlife Refuge, Ma'alea Harbor, Molokini Island

afternoon. Wailea and Kihei are not as affected by this cloud cover, and I will photograph those later in the day, when the water is more blue.

In the middle of the day I usually put the camera down and go swimming or take a nap. I will wait until about 3 P.M. before I start again. The crowds start to thin out on the beaches, and there are numerous sites from which to photograph sunset.

South Maui is really all about the beaches. It's not possible to shoot, or even see, all of them in one day. Pick a few, take your time, and don't forget your sunscreen.

La Perouse Bay (38)

La Perouse Bay is named after Jean-Francois de Galaup de La Perouse, the French explorer who was the first European to land on Maui. To get to La Perouse Bay you simply drive to the end of the road. However there is no beach. Snorkeling is not that good here either. This is the site of the last volcanic activity on Maui, in

An aerial view of La Perouse Bay

Ahihi Cove

1790, so it's mainly black lava rubble. There are some archeological sites that may be of interest to photograph, however they are not really that distinct.

There are some spots great for snorkeling and fair photos in between La Perouse and Ahihi Cove that require about 30 minutes of hiking. It may be a good idea to study the Google Earth satellite photo before you go and don't forget good shoes and plenty of water. No facilities.

Directions: Take Makena Road all the way to the end. The last mile or so will be very narrow. It ends at a gravel parking lot by the water.

Ahihi Cove (39)

Ahihi Cove is a spot that is usually protected from wind and waves, so it's one of the best snorkeling spots on Maui. It is a very picturesque small bay where the reef comes up to the shore. Because the reef is so close to shore, this is a good area to use a polarizing filter. It will make the reef stand out and the water seem even clearer. If you walk around on the rocks here, be careful; they are very slippery.

There is no beach and very limited parking. No facilities.

Directions: Ahihi Cove is toward the end of Makena Road, past the Ahihi-Kinau Reserve sign.

Pa'ako Beach (40)

Pa'ako Beach is also known as Secret Cove. It's just past the end of Makena Beach going out. You will see a blue shoreline access sign and an opening in the wall. Swimming and snorkeling

Makena Beach

Makena Beach (41)

Makena Beach, also known as Big Beach, is big, about a mile long and over 100 yards wide. It's also one of the most beautiful places on Maui, and one of the most popular. It used to be fairly deserted but is very crowded now, especially on weekends. If you want to spend the day, arrive early. If you show up late you may have to hike a half a mile to get to the beach.

The beach itself is excellent for swimming and snorkeling. At the north end you will see a point and a cliff. The cliff is the best place to photograph the beach from, and it can be good in both morning and afternoon light. You'll have to climb up, which is not too difficult but it is good to have both hands free.

People will be also climbing over this all day to get to Little Beach, which is Maui's famous nude beach. Photography is not recommended or appreciated there. It's a nice place to take a swim though.

Portable toilets are the only facilities here.

Directions: Out past the resort areas of Wailea and Makena you'll see a crater (Pu'u Olai) out by the sea. Makena Beach is on the other side. There will be a turnoff into a paved lot that will be full if you're not early. However there is other parking in dirt lots and on the road.

Little Beach (42)

Little Beach (Pu'u Olai) has been Maui's unofficial nude beach for decades. Nudity is officially illegal in Hawaii but apparently the hundreds of people who come here each week don't know that. On weekends it is unbelievably crowded. No photography please. *Take only photographs and leave only footprints* does not work here, however you could sneak a couple of wide shots from up on the cliff.

Directions: Use the same directions as for Makena Beach for parking. When you get to

should be good, but stay out if the sea is rough. It's also a good spot to explore and photograph some of the coastline. However, you may come across a wedding, or at least wedding photography, here. It happens almost every day.

Parking is very limited and there are no facilities.

Directions: On the way out to the end of the road, just past Makena Beach, you will see a rock wall with a blue shoreline access sign. There is only room for about three cars but you can park farther up the road.

the beach, go all the way to the right to climb over the cliff onto Little Beach.

Oneuli Beach (43)

Sometimes called Black Sand Beach it maybe should be called grey sand beach because it is nowhere near as black as Wai'anapanapa in Hana. You can't see this beach from the road so most people drive right on by. Snorkeling can be good if the water is calm and you get out and to the left.

This is an interesting beach to photograph in both directions. Looking left it is backed by the cliff and cone of Pu'u Olai. To the right you're looking all the way down the coastline to the West Maui Mountains. The color of the sand changes as you move down the beach as well.

Directions: Access is kind of hard to find. It's a turnoff where Makena Alanui turns into Makena Road. You'll see the cinder cone. If you get to Makena Beach, you have gone too far. It's a dirt road; you go down and to the right. It's usually passable without four-wheel drive, unless it's raining.

Malu'aka Beach (44)

Malu'aka is known by a number of different names, including Turtle Beach. It's the beach right in front of the Maui Prince Resort. Because the hotel is set back a way, the beach feels somewhat secluded. It's good for swimming and snorkeling, and home to many sea turtles. The best area is to the left. The resort operates a concession on the beach where you can rent equipment, get a snack, or book a sailboat ride. It's a good beach for families.

Malu'aka is also one of my favorite places to photograph the sunset. There are both coconut palms and kiawe trees with which to frame the setting sun. The water is usually calm and the island of Lanai sits off in the distance.

Malu'aka is also much less crowded at sunset than nearby Wailea and Makena beaches. Restrooms and showers are available.

Directions: Coming from Wailea on Wailea Alanui Drive go past the Makena Beach Resort and take the first right. This will take you to a parking lot; it's a short walk down to the beach from there.

Oneuli Beach

Pro Tip: When the sun goes down behind the horizon, the sunset is not over! It can last for about another 30 minutes. As the light dims, the scene shifts through many colors. The effect can be quite stunning, particularly with calm water and islands on the horizon. A few clouds are better than none, as well. A slow shutter speed of a couple of seconds or more can create a surreal feeling of movement in the water.

Keawalai Congregational Church in Makena

The light-capturing ability of new digital sensors makes it possible to capture light you really can't even see. If you keep shooting exposures past when it looks good to your eyes, you'll find out what I mean. Of course you need a tripod (and a patient spouse or traveling companion).

Makena Landing (45)

Makena Landing is along the old Makena Road. It goes along a series of small coves surrounded by kiawe (mesquite) trees. This is very calm water, good for both snorkeling and kayaking. On Makena Road is the lava rock Keawalai Congregational Church, which dates from 1832. Both the church and the cemetery are interesting to photograph.

Directions: If you're coming from Wailea, turn to the right onto Makena Road at the end of the golf course. If you miss that turn, you can turn right at Honoiki Street and it will go down to Makena Road. If you get to Makena Beach Resort you have gone too far.

Po'olenalena Beach (46)

Po'olenalena Beach, like other beaches in the area, has blue water and white sand. This beach is very long and wide and less crowded than its neighbors in Wailea. The swimming is good and sometimes there are even small waves for bodyboarding. Snorkeling in the area around the rocks can be excellent when the water is calm.

Directions: The main access is at the north end of the beach. It's a dirt parking lot but there is plenty of space. At the south end you'll see an access sign at the Makena Surf. There is a small parking lot there and a walkway to a beautiful section of the beach. I prefer to photograph the beach from the end looking toward West Maui.

Palauea Beach

Palauea Beach (47)

This beach is much like Poʻolenelena right next to it. It's uncrowded, especially during the week. The calm water, the blues and whites of ocean and sand, make it a great place to spend the day, though it may not be as photogenic as other spots nearby.

There are no facilities (unless you count the portalet).

Directions: From Wailea turn right onto Kaukahi Street just past Kea Lani Resort, then turn left on Makena Road. After the first curve you'll see an empty lot and probably the portalet. Park by the road and follow the path through the trees.

Polo Beach (48)

Polo Beach, at the south end of Wailea, is right in front of the Kea Lani Resort and can be crowded all day long. The beach is not as attractive as others in Wailea. Snorkeling can be good, especially to the right, however it can get windy here. The hotel has a concession that offers outrigger canoe rides from here so you can often photograph them offshore. There are showers and restrooms.

Directions: From Wailea turn right onto Kaukahi Street just past Kea Lani. Go down toward the beach; the parking will be on the left. Then follow the access signs to the beach.

Wailea Beach (49)

Wailea Beach sits right in front of the huge Grand Wailea Resort and the Four Seasons Resort, and it's always full of people from both. Parking is limited and away from the beach. If you're not staying here it's easier to go to Ulua or Mokapu beaches nearby.

Photography here and at Ulua or Mokapu beaches is best early or late in the day. Wailea Beach is my favorite for sunset photos, though, because of the number and alignment of the coconut palms.

Wailea Beach

Directions: The beach is right in front of the Grand Wailea Resort on Wailae Alanui Drive. There is a small amount of public parking in between the Grand Wailea and Four Seasons, with a walkway to the beach.

Ulua Beach (50)

Ulua Beach is right in middle of Wailea Resort. It's next to Mokapu Beach and they share the same parking, restrooms, and showers. Ulua may be the most popular of Wailea beaches but for me it's the least photogenic (though still beautiful to be at). It's known to be the best for body surfing or bodyboarding but when calm is also a snorkeling spot.

Directions: Drive down Wailea Alanui Drive and turn toward the ocean at Hale Alii Place. There will be a beach access sign. Park and go left to Ulua Beach or right to Mokapu Beach.

Mokapu Beach (51)

Mokapu Beach is right next to Ulua Beach. It used to have the Renaissance Wailea Resort behind it, but something new is coming up. Mokapu means "forbidden place" in Hawaiian but obviously a lot of people don't know that.

I like to photograph this beach from the south end in the morning. I like the curve of the beach with mountains in the background.

Directions: Drive down Wailea Alanui Drive and turn toward the ocean at Hale Alii Place. There will be a beach access sign. Park and go left to Ulua Beach or right to Mokapu Beach.

Pro Tip: The parking lot between Mokapu and Ulua is the start of the Wailea Beach Walk and you can hike past Wailea Beach all the way to Polo Beach. These are all good white sand beaches with clear blue water. For photography I will park in this lot. There are about 50 spaces, but they fill up early.

I like to travel light when I photograph

beaches. It can get very hot trudging across the sand with a large backpack. During the day I usually take one camera and two lenses, a wide-angle zoom (16–35mm) and a telephoto zoom (70–200mm). Really early or late in the day I will go ahead and bring the whole backpack, along with a tripod

Another thing I do is try to plan ahead by getting that gear out of my backpack and storing the backpack in the trunk before I get to my parking place. That way when I get out of the car I am not fumbling with a lot of equipment and possibly becoming a target for thieves. Break-ins are not a huge problem in most places on Maui but they certainly do happen

Keawakapu Beach (52)

Keawakapu is on the north end of Wailea. It's a very long beach with a sandy bottom that is usually perfect for swimming. As with all of this coast, the wind is lighter early or late, so those are the best times to visit or photograph. This beach is usually less crowded than others north or south.

Directions: There are three entrances, but I recommend the one at the very south end of South Kihei Road. Just keep driving on Kihei Road toward Wailea, and when it curves up the hill go straight to the end. The parking, restrooms, and showers are there, and I like this

Mokapu Beach

Kamaole Beach Park 3

section of the beach. There is also a parking lot in the middle of the beach at the corner of South Kihei Road and Kilohana. Look for the blue access sign.

DIVERSION: Kihei Coastal Trail

Running between Keawakapu Beach and Kamaole Beach Park 3 is a short hike called Kihei Coastal Trail. This is a good place to get away from the beach crowds. It's not as stunning or dramatic as other shoreline hikes, but you will see some birds (mainly shearwaters) and native plants. There are some benches along the way and signs to explain the flora. About halfway through the hike you cross the boat ramp. This is not something I would make a special trip to, but it may be worth taking in if you're in the area.

Kamaole Beach Park 3 (53)

Kamaole Beach Park 3 is one of three beach parks called Kamaole that are close to each other in Kihei. They are all very similar and have good facilities, including lifeguards, restrooms, and showers. Each has parking, but it's a good idea to get here early because these beaches are very popular.

Beach number 3 has the largest park, with several picnic tables. There are a couple of low palm trees that are good for framing sunset or day photos.

Directions: All three Kamaole Beach parks are right on the South Kihei Road. This one is closest to Wailea and right in front of the Kamaole Sands.

Kamaole Beach Park 1

Kamaole Beach Park 2 (54)

Kamaole Beach Park 2 is the smallest beach of the three, but because of the nearby rocks is probably the best for snorkeling. Swimming is usually very good as well. When there is a little bit of surf you can bodyboard or body surf.

Directions: All three Kamaole Beach parks are right on the South Kihei Road.

Kamaole Beach Park 1 (55)

Kamaole Beach Park 1 is the largest and possibly the nicest of the three. It stretches quite a way; in fact the north end of it is often referred to as Charley Young Beach.

Swimming here is usually very good, while snorkeling is better at no. 2. When there is a little bit of surf you can bodyboard or body surf.

This beach is my favorite of the three to photograph, though. There are numerous angles, in both directions and out on the point, to shoot from morning and afternoon. It's an excellent place to photograph the sunset and afterglow.

Directions: All three Kamaole Beach parks are right on the South Kihei Road. This is the first one you'll get to if you're headed south. There is an ABC store right across the street if you need supplies.

DIVERSION: Hawaiian Islands Humpback Whale National Marine Sanctuary

Hawaiian Islands Humpback Whale National Marine Sanctuary encompasses the main Hawaiian islands; its Learning Center, an interesting and worthwhile stop, is on Maui. The beachfront education center has artifacts, exhibits, and a library. Every Tuesday and Thursday at 11:00 A.M. they have whale talks. This is a good place for families and, best of all, it's free (http://hawaiihumpbackwhale.noaa.gov/welcome.html; 800-831-4888).

Directions: The marine sanctuary is at 726 S. Kihei Rd.

Sugar Beach (56)

This 3-mile stretch of sand goes across Ma'alaea Bay. If you like long walks on the beach, this is your place. It's called Sugar Beach because the sand is so fine. It's often windy in the middle of the day, making this beach popular with windsurfers and kiteboarders. Several outrigger canoe clubs use the north end beach as a storage and launch site as well. Because of all this it's a good place to shoot water sports. Sailors will be out in the afternoon; when the wind dies, the outrigger canoes start launching. It's also another excellent sunset spot.

Directions: The part of the beach where you'll find the canoes is near the beginning of South Kihei Road right after it splits off from North Kihei Road (HI 31). It's right next to Kihei Beach Condominiums. You will be able to see the outrigger canoes from the road.

Outrigger canoes on Sugar Beach

Napili Bay

V. West Maui

General Description: West Maui covers the area from just past Ma'alaea Harbor to past Kahakuloa. Most notably it includes Lahaina and the resort areas of Kaanapali, Napili, and Kapalua. Most of these spots are along the shoreline; there are really not many roads that go very far up into the mountains. Napali and Kahekili are some of the most beautiful beaches in Hawaii. The town and harbor of Lahaina is full of photographic opportunities all day and into the evening. Farther down the coast, Bellstone Pools, Nakalele Blowhole, and the community of Kahakuloa are all very interesting.

Where: The west side of the West Maui Mountains from McGregor Point past Lahaina, Kaanapali, Kapalua out to Kahakuloa. There is only one road, Honoapiilani Highway (HI 30), which passes through all of these places. You can actually take the road past Kahakuloa all the way back around to Wailuku. There is not much to see or photograph on that section, though, so I only recommend it if you wanted to go to Wailuku anyway.

Noted For: The resorts and beaches of Kaanapali, Kapalua and Napili, as well as the historic and photogenic town of Lahaina. Lahaina is also known for its art galleries, restaurants, and bars. West Maui is also a high activity area with lots of surfing, snorkeling, diving, parasailing, golfing, whale watching, and outrigger canoe paddling.

Best Times: West Maui, like most of the island, is best photographed early or late. However, the West Maui Mountains block the light in the morning so there is no point in getting out at dawn. Sunsets are best from Launiupoko Beach Park around to Kapalua Beach.

Facilities: Most beach parks have restrooms and showers, though a few, such as Papalaua Wayside Park, only have portalets. In the resort areas there are surprising few public facilities. This is especially true of Kaanapali. It seems the county planners were asleep during its permitting process. Fortunately later resorts such as Kapalua, Wailea, and Makena are a bit friendlier as far as public access, parking and facilities are concerned.

Parking: It's not too difficult, with the exceptions of Kaanapali, Lahaina Town, and Kapalua. Resort beach parking can be crowded from about 10 A.M. to 3 P.M. After that people start moving toward Lahaina, and between 4 P.M. and 8 P.M. it's hard to find a spot there.

Sleeps and Eats: Too many to name. The resorts all have excellent hotels, condos, and restaurants. Two of my favorite places to stay are the Napili Kai Resort and Royal Lahaina Resort (which is actually in Kaanapali).

My favorite restaurants include The Sea House at Napili Kai for dinner. It's right on the water, so get there while it's still light. The Gazebo in Napili and the Plantation House in Kapalua are excellent for breakfast. In Kaanapali I like Hula Grill for lunch, dinner, or hanging out at the bar. In Lahaina I recommend Mala Ocean Tavern and Lahaina Grill. There is also a great happy hour with food and drinks in the bar at Ruth's Chris Steak House.

Sites Included: Papalaua Wayside Park, Olowalu, Launiupoko Beach Park, Lahaina Beach, Lahaina Harbor, Lahaina Town, Hanakao'o Beach Park, Kaanapali, Kahekili Beach, Napili Bay, Kapalua Beach, Mokuleia Bay, Honolua Bay, Nakalele Blowhole, Bellstone Pools, Kahakuloa Town

West Maui is a bit different from South Maui, and if you look at a map you'll see why. The coastline of South Maui is fairly straight, so there I tend to start at one end and work my way around. West Maui bends around a half circle. Nearer Ma'alaea the shoreline points south. At Lahaina and Kaanapali it points due west, which makes these locations the best for sunsets. Up at Kapalua and farther along, the shoreline starts to point north.

All of this means that when I photograph West Maui, I tend to jump around a lot. There are also weather considerations. On days when the trade winds blow, it's almost always sunny from Ma'alaea to Lahaina. Starting around 9 A.M. or 10 A.M., there is a line of clouds that often descends on the edge of Kaanapali though Kapalua. On most days these clouds will dissipate by late afternoon. I was once doing a shoot for a production company on the best beaches in America. There was a film crew complete with models, assistants, makeup, etc. We were at Kapalua when it clouded up around 2 P.M. the director said, "That's it. We're done for the day." I told him I was sure it would clear back up if he would wait an hour. "Nope," he said, "we're done." It was sunny and beautiful by the time I drove my car out of the parking lot.

The point is, weather changes quickly on Maui, and especially on West Maui. Generally

Papalaua Wayside Park

Olowalu petroglyphs

my advice is to photograph the north and south sections in the morning and the middle (Lahaina to Napili) in the afternoon. However there are great morning opportunities from Lahaina to Napili as well. The water is calm, the ocean is blue, and the islands of Lanai and Molokai are floating off in the distance. It's hard to go wrong.

Papalaua Wayside Park (57)

There are a number of spots along the road from Ma'alaea to Lahaina to pull off the road by the beach. Papalaua Wayside Park is the closest one to Ma'alaea. Second is Ukumehame State Park. There are also other places to park that are not state parks and they are just as good. The only facilities these state parks offer are portalets and you probably don't really want to go in one of those on a hot, sunny day anyhow.

On this shore you'll see people surfing, stand-up boarding, picnicking, and snorkeling.

It's an easy place to learn to surf, but be careful about going too far offshore. If you get into the wind line, it can be very hard to get back. People have drowned on this coast for that very reason.

Photographically, the beaches here are not that scenic, but the activity is constant, close, and therefore easy to shoot.

Directions: Papalaua Wayside Park is on HI 30 between the mile markers 11 and 12. Ukumehame State Park is about a mile farther up the road. There is plenty of parking at both.

Olowalu (58)

Olowalu is a small historic town. It was originally a Hawaiian village and was the site of a terrible massacre. In 1790 Captain Simon Metcalfe had a small boat stolen. In retaliation he decided to lure the islanders out to his ship for trading. When the canoes approached, he opened fire with cannon and muskets, killing over 100.

Sunset at Launiupoko Beach Park

the north side. Go up that road about half a mile; look for a red railing and the remains of a stairway on the right side. It's not really a very pleasant hike, so I only recommend it for those who want the see the petroglyphs. The early afternoon would be best for light.

Directions: Olowalu is at mile marker 15 on HI 30. You can park by the Olowalu General Store.

Launiupoko Beach Park (59)

Launiupoko Beach in a small roadside park just outside of Lahaina. It's popular with families because of an area protected by a seawall that makes a great spot for kids to swim. Launiupoko is also an excellent place to picnic, and there's good surfing right off the point.

It is very much like Papalaua Wayside Park and other spots along the coast with one exception. This park has coconut palm trees along the shore. That makes it one of my favorite spots to photograph sunsets on Maui. There will be people all around, so it's possible to get silhouettes of surfers carrying boards. The island of Lanai is offshore, and sometimes it will be backlit with the suns rays coming though it.

Directions: Launiupoko Beach Park is on HI 30 just before you get to Lahaina. There is a good-size parking lot there along with restrooms, showers, and picnic tables.

Lahaina Beach (60)

Most people don't even know Lahaina Beach exists. It starts just south of Lahaina Harbor. Most days you'll see surfers riding small waves or getting lessons. Neither the sand nor the water is very good here, so I do not recommend it for swimming, snorkeling, or spending the day. There are much better places in West Maui for that.

In the mid 1800s the area became a plantation town and Chinese, Japanese, and Portuguese were brought in to work the fields. There was a landing at the point, and steamships delivered freight, passengers, and mail.

Almost everything is gone now. Even the plantation houses were moved. There is a store and a very good restaurant under the trees. Nearby are some of the best petroglyphs in Hawaii, though they are hard to find. There is a road behind the Olowalu General Store on

Lahaina Beach can be a good place to photograph or take a stroll late in the day though. There is plenty of activity. The sun sets behind Lanai, and I will often photograph this area and the harbor in the same walk.

Directions: Lahaina Beach starts just south of the harbor, so it's easiest if you park near the harbor. You can also get to the beach through Kamehameha Iki Park (no parking), or the 505 Front Street Shopping Center.

Lahaina Harbor (61)

Lahaina Harbor is the center of activity in this area. It is from here that you can join whale watch cruises, snorkeling cruises, trips to Molokai or Lanai, or book a fishing charter. There are two lines of boat slips that are a mix of commercial and private vessels. These are not the large, sleek yachts of Miami or Marina del Rey. Most of these boats are fairly beaten up, but that makes them more interesting to photograph.

Right behind the harbor are several historic buildings. The green Pioneer Inn is still a hotel and has a good bar. The largest banyan tree in Hawaii is also there. I don't think you can miss it. It doesn't look as if it's all one tree but it is.

I always photograph the harbor late in the day. I will walk up and down the front line of boats and photograph the Pioneer Inn and Lahaina Courthouse. I will then go out to the far docks so I can shoot back in toward the boats to get the mountains in the background. There are two ways to do this: The first and easiest is to stay on the docks; it works fine and will take you to several good vantage

Lahaina Harbor

points. The second is to cross over to the rocks to get farther out. This is better but it's slow going and, of course, riskier. If the rocks are wet, don't do it; if they're dry, be careful.

Directions: When you see the giant banyan tree on Front Street, you're there. I often have luck driving around the banyan tree and finding a free parking spot. There is also a free lot one block south at Prison Street.

DIVERSION: Submarine ride

Like Maui Ocean Center this is another way to get underwater photos without getting wet. Atlantis Submarines (www.atlantisadventures .com; 800-548-6262) offers tours on Maui, Oahu, and the Big Island. On Maui they operate out of Lahaina, carry 48 passengers, and dive down to about 100 feet. Recently the Carthaginian, a replica of a whaling ship that had been moored at Laihana Harbor for decades, was sunk offshore. It created an artificial reef that makes for incredible viewing of marine life. The voyage is highly recommended, unless you're claustrophobic.

Pro Tip: I have a couple of photo tips for the submarine ride. Don't use your flash, as the

A humpback whale tail

light will just bounce back off the glass. There isn't much light down deep, so you'll need to raise the ISO setting on your camera to 400 or 800. Finally, your photos will probably still look too blue. If you have Photoshop, go to Image on the menu, drop down to Adjustments, and over to Auto Color. Auto Color has never worked for me with anything else, but for over-blue underwater shots it is amazing.

Pro Tip: Lahaina was the whaling capital of the world from 1825 to 1860. In some ways it still is. Of course, now the object is to see and maybe shoot them (with cameras, not harpoons). The season for humpback whales is November to May, though your best bet is December to early April. The whales come in to give birth, and approximately 2,000 show up in Maui's waters each year. Therefore it's not hard to see them. Getting good photographs is another matter. I know photographers who have worked the whale watch boats for years and only have a couple of dozen excellent photos to show.

That doesn't mean you shouldn't try though, and I think the best bet is to take a whale watch tour out of Lahaina Harbor. If you go early or very late in the day the chances are better that the wind and waves will be calm. Shop around and look at the boat. I prefer something bigger with shade. This keeps me from getting fried and my gear from getting soaked.

When you get out there, the urge is to photograph with the longest telephoto lens you have. I have missed a lot of shots that way. By the time I compose and lock focus, the whale is gone. It's better to use a zoom, wide to telephoto, or a regular telephoto lens. Start with it at the widest. Find the whale, then zoom in. Breaching whales are almost impossible to predict and catch on film. Tail slaps and fin slaps are easier. When you see the tail go straight up

A banyan tree in Lahaina

and slip into the water, the whale is diving. You won't see that whale again for a while.

Lahaina Town (62)

Lahaina is one of the most historic towns in the islands. It was the capital of the Kingdom of Hawaii from 1820 to 1845. For most of the 19th century it was the center of the Pacific whaling fleet and was full of bars and brothels. Today there are still a lot of bars along with restaurants, shops, museums, and art galleries. About two million people a year visit Lahaina, so be prepared for crowds. Front Street, which runs along the ocean, is the main drag. There is some parking along the road, but you will probably have to go into one of the lots at the ends.

I tend to like to park at the harbor end and work my way up. The historic Baldwin Home and Masters Reading room are right across the street. Then there is a section of the street that

Baldwin Home, Lahaina

is open on the ocean side; there are some two-story wooden buildings across from it. This area is best photographed in the late afternoon from either end of the street. Farther down the street, I like to photograph the Wo Hing Society Hall. It was built in 1912 and restored in 1984. There are some exhibits but the interiors and exteriors of the building are the most interesting to see and walk around.

When Front Street opens up again, you are at the Lahaina Center, where the Hard Rock Café and Ruth's Chris Steak House are. This is where I usually end my walk, sometimes right at sunset because there is a line of coconut palms along the bulkhead here.

Most of what is interesting is on Front Street. One block back, however, on Wainee Street, you can find a couple of old churches, the Seamen's Cemetery, a Hongwanji mission, and the old Lahaina Prison.

Directions: Lahaina is on HI 30, also known as Honoapiilani Highway. It's hard to miss; when you see the old sugar mill tower, turn toward the ocean on Lahainaluna Road. That will take you right down to the middle of Front Street. If you turn left and are very lucky, you can find free parking on Front Street. Otherwise drive down to find a space at the harbor. Just past the harbor at the corner of Front Street and Prison Street is a public lot that is free for three hours. There are also pay lots scattered around.

DIVERSION: Friday Art Night

Every Friday night is Art Night in Lahaina. Art galleries are a big business in Lahaina, and there are dozens of them. Most are on Front Street but a few are also on Lahainaluna Road. The official hours are 7 P.M. to 10 P.M. but you may want to show up earlier for parking and the sunset. Stroll around and you'll see plenty of activity in both the galleries and bars. It's also a good opportunity to shoot twilight and night photos.

Hanakaoʻo Beach Park (63)

Hanakaoʻo Beach Park is at the Lahaina end of Kaanapali Resort. It is also known as Canoe Beach. The sand here is not as fine and white as at Kaanapali, and the water is not as good for swimming. This park is used mainly for picnics. Most every afternoon you will see canoe clubs practicing, and occasionally you will see canoe races happening here. This—along with Kanaha Beach in Central Maui and Sugar Beach on the South Shore—is the best place to photograph outrigger canoes.

Directions: Hanakaoʻo Beach Park is on HI 30 just on the Lahaina side of Kaanapali Beach. In fact it is the very south end of Kaanapali Beach.

There is a large parking lot, restrooms, showers, and picnic tables.

Kaanapali Beach (64)

Kaanapali Beach is one of Hawaii's best. Several hotels in Kaanapali Resort are on the beachfront, as is the Whalers Village shopping center. This is a long beach that is excellent for swimming and snorkeling. There are several places to eat or rent equipment.

It's a hard beach to get to if you're not staying at one of the hotels. There are no facilities, but you can go into a nearby hotel or the Whalers Village, which is toward the center of the beach. Whalers Village may be the best

Hanakaoʻo Beach Park

Kaanapali Beach

place to park as well, but it's expensive. A few free parking spots are set aside at each hotel for "beach access," and if you get there very early maybe you can get one of those. The Kaanapali Beach Hotel usually has the least expensive paid parking, which was $10 for the day at last report.

I like to photograph this beach either from in front of the shopping center looking toward Black Rock Point or from Black Rock looking in the other direction. The beach on the south side of the shopping center gets narrow, with more waves, reef, and darker sand. Kaanapali is beautiful in the morning or at sunset looking out across sailboats toward Lanai or Molokai.

Directions: Kaanapali is off HI 30. You turn into it at Kaanapali Parkway. You can see the resorts from the highway. Parking is difficult and is described above.

DIVERSION: Sunset Cliff Dive and Hula Show

Every day at sunset there is a torch-lighting ceremony and cliff dive at Black Rock. It may not be as spectacular or daring as in Acapulco, but it is more scenic.

You can also wander over to the Kaanapali Beach Hotel for some Hawaiian music and hula dancing out near the pool. This is not spectacular either but it's genuine fun, and free (except for drinks).

Kahekili Beach (65)

Some consider Kahekili Beach to be part of Kaanapali Beach. It's also sometimes called North Beach, but its real name is Kahekili and it was named after the last king of Maui. It stretches from the other side of Black Rock for about 2 miles. There is a great public park at the north end with lots of parking, restrooms, and tables. The water is about the same as at Kaanapali but may be a little calmer and clearer. Swimming is great, as is snorkeling offshore. It's usually best in the morning as the wind picks up during the day. It's also better to go off to the left toward Kaanapali. There are fewer rocks.

This is a great place to watch and photograph the sunset and twilight. While not empty, it is certainly less crowded than Kaanapali Beach.

Directions: From HI 30 just past mile marker 25 turn left onto Kai Ala Drive. This will take you right down to the park.

Napili Bay (66)

Napili Beach is one of my favorites. It's on a beautiful bay between Kaanapali and Kapalua. Napili Bay is excellent for swimming and snorkeling. There are condos and hotels all along the beach, so you won't be alone, but it's not terribly crowded either.

As at most beaches, the best time to be at Napili is early or late in the day. Not too early here though, because it takes time for the sun to clear the mountains. It's another spectacular sunset location, and depending on the time of year you can go out a walkway on the north end to shoot twilight.

A couple of my favorite places to eat on

Kahekili Beach

Maui are here. For breakfast go to the Gazebo Restaurant on the south end of the beach. They are busy, so you'll probably have to wait. I also like the Sea House Restaurant in Napili Kai Resort for dinner. Sometimes I just sit at the bar, order appetizers, and watch the waves.

Directions: From Lahaina on HI 30 turn left on Napilihau Street, which is just past mile marker 29. Take this down to Lower Hono-apiilani Road and turn right. There may be parking to the left on Napili Place or Hui Drive, but that's unlikely. If you drive farther around the bay to just past Napili Kai Resort you'll find a public lot with restrooms and showers nearby. This is a good place to park for either Napili Beach or Kapalua Beach, as it's right between the two.

Kapalua Beach (67)

The Kapalua Resort surrounds Kapalua Beach. There is free parking and right of way to the beach, though. It's a good beach for swimming and snorkeling, though I prefer Napili right around the point. This a fantastic place to watch and photograph the sunset, and for that it's probably better than Napili. The beach is backed by coconut palms that are good to shoot in either direction. The rocky point is also a good place to take very long exposures at the end of twilight.

Kapalua Beach

Directions: Use the same route and parking tips as for Napili Beach.

DIVERSION: Luaus

I would like to give you an in-depth review of all the luaus on Maui but, honestly, I have not been to any of them. When you live in the islands, you tend to skip such things. That doesn't mean they aren't worthwhile, and I have been to a couple on Oahu and had fun. Here's a great website that reviews Maui luaus: www.mauihawaiiluau.com. Their recommendations seem good.

From a photographer's perspective, I think the Old Lahaina Luau definitely has the best location. It's next to the water with palm trees and you can watch the sun setting behind Molokai and Lanai. It's also supposedly a bit more authentic. I have been on the beach at sunset while the Wailea, Kaanapali, and Sheraton luaus were happening, and it looked like all were having a good time.

If you are not interested in a full luau, there is Hawaiian music and hula dancing at Kaanapali Beach Hotel every night at about sunset. It's kind of a mini luau without the food, but you can order drinks and food. The show is free. It takes place in a grass shack stage in front of palm trees, so photographic opportunities are good.

If you are not interested in luaus at all you may want to consider Warren & Annabelle's Magic Show on Front Street in Lahaina. It's a nightly small gathering with cocktails, appetizers, and dessert followed by a two hours of magic. The show has more humor than hype and is highly recommended.

DIVERSION: Kapalua Coastal Trail

The Kapalua Coastal Trail and Boardwalk runs from Oneloa Beach to Kapalua Beach. The area in front of Oneloa Beach is a nice wide boardwalk. It goes out to a rocky point

A sunset hula show in Kaanapali

with a lava formation known as the Dragon's Teeth. Past the point is Namalu Bay, which is excellent for snorkeling when it's calm. Just past the next point is Kapalua Beach. When I hike here, I park at the lot between Kapalua Beach and Napili Beach and do a round-trip. It can be good to photograph either early or late in the day.

Mokuleia Bay (68)

Mokuleia Bay is a great spot. It's sometimes called Slaughterhouse Beach because they used to slaughter cattle nearby. Now it's just a very protected beach set at the bottom of a cliff. You have to hike down a short path to get to it. The cliff shields the beach from trade winds and makes it much more calm and pleasant than nearby Fleming Beach. The short hike down also thins out the crowd, as does the limited parking. It's best to get here early both for parking and photographs.

Directions: Mokuleia Bay is at mile marker 32 on HI 30. There is not much parking, but you can pull off farther down the road and walk back.

Honolua Bay

Honolua Bay (69)

Honolua has no beach. The center of the bay is made up of rocks, pebbles, and some rough sand. It's a marine preserve that is excellent for snorkeling in the summer.

In the winter the surf picks up. With a northwest swell Honolua Bay is the best surfing spot on Maui. It's for experts only because the waves break hard in very shallow water. You'll see cars parked along the cliffs on the right hand side. This is where you want to go to photograph the surfing. There are several spots where you can set up and shoot down on the waves. Be careful; it can be slippery climbing around there, especially with gear in you hands. You can get pretty close though, and a short telephoto will be all you need. I often try to do some motion pans here and find that 1/8 to 1/30 second exposures work well and a tripod will greatly improve the odds for success.

Directions: About 1/2 mile past mile marker 32 you can park and walk a short path to the shore. This is where you want to be in the summer for snorkeling or swimming. To photograph surfing or the bay you need to keep driving around the bay. You'll see a dirt road that goes out toward the point. If there's any surf, there will be a number of cars on it. Park out there and carefully find your spot to shoot from.

Nakalele Blowhole (70)

Nakalele Blowhole is a natural waterspout on a very rugged section of northwest Maui's coastline. It's a very interesting area to hike around; I like the area to the left of the blowhole best. There are lava shelves up here with some of the most jagged erosion I have ever seen. You do not want to slip and fall.

Directions: Park about halfway between mile markers 38 and 39 and hike down to the shore. It's a short trail but it's steep and you'll need good shoes, definitely not rubber slippers. About halfway down you should see the blowhole. If the seas are calm it might not be going off, but go down anyway.

Bellstone Pools (71)

Bellstone Pools, also known as Olivine Pools, are probably the most spectacular tidal pools in Hawaii. They are accessible via a relatively short but fairly steep hike from the road. Again, you need good shoes because there are plenty of opportunities to slip and fall. If you want to swim in the pools, wear your shoes into the water. The only swimming is in the tide pools, and even that can be very dangerous if the surf is big. People have been washed away here, so be very careful.

Bellstone Pools

These can be photographed any time of day. You'll see into the pools better in the middle of the day if you use a polarizing filter. The rock formations and erosion will look better early or late in the day. There is also a smaller pool off to the right around the first point, but it's even harder to climb down to and is more exposed to the wave action.

Kahakuloa Village

Directions: If you're coming from Lahaina Park about 3/4 of a mile after mile marker 42 and just before the next mile marker, which for some reason is 16. There are several trails down but if you see a yellow danger sign, you know you're in the right place. It's down and a little to the left of that. Know and respect your own physical limitations; please hike with caution.

Kahakuloa (72)

The farther you drive on HI 340, the narrower the road becomes. Eventually you come around a bend and see Kahakuloa Village. This is a small community of about 100 people. The little green wooden church still occasionally has services in Hawaiian. There is a tropical garden and a couple of art studios as well as stands that sell fresh fruit and banana bread.

The village is best photographed from the road descending right above the church or from the other side, where the road rises and just before it turns out of the valley. The road is very narrow in both places, so be sure to get your car completely out of the way before you leave it.

Directions: HI 30 turns into HI 340 just before Kahakuloa. The village is between mile markers 14 and 15. You can't miss it because it's the only thing even close to a town on this coastline.

DIVERSION: Molokai and Lanai

Day trips to Molokai or Lanai are an option you should consider if you have the time. They are both very different and quite interesting. Both islands are part of Maui county. Many of the workers in Maui resorts make the commute every day by boat from Kauanakakai Harbor and Manele Bay.

Of the two, Molokai is by far more photogenic. It's 38 miles long and about 10 miles wide. While that may sound easy to cover in a day, it really is not. If you fly in or come by boat

A mule ride on Molokai

you'll land in pretty much the center of the island near the main town of Kauanakakai. You could head west to the rather run down resort area of Kuluakoi. The hotel is closed, the golf course is overgrown with weeds, but the beaches are still there and they are beautiful. This whole end of the island is quite dry though, and if you're spending only one day on Molokai, I recommend heading east all the way to the end of the road in Halawa Valley. This is one of the most scenic drives in Hawaii.

Another possibility is taking a day tour of Kalaupapa. Kalaupapa is the remote peninsula off the north shore of Molokai. Molokai has the highest sea cliffs in the world, and the Kalau-

papa Peninsula juts out in the middle of them. The fact that it's so remote and inaccessible made it the choice for a leper colony location back in the 1860s. Lepers were brought from all over Hawaii and literally dumped offshore and abandoned. Many did not live long. Father Damien, who was recently canonized, came over in 1873. He built churches, homes, and a hospital. He also started farms and an irrigation system. Mother Marianne, who is also up for sainthood, joined him in 1888. With their help and guidance a community was built. Father Damien contracted the disease in 1876 and died from it at Kalaupapa in 1879. Mother Marianne stayed there till she was 78 years old.

A catamaran off Lanai

Today leprosy is called Hanson's Disease and it is contained and controlled by drugs. Several patients still live in Kalaupapa and have the right to for the rest of their days. The whole peninsula is now a national park. There are tours daily except Sunday. You can fly into the peninsula by calling Damien Tours (808-567-6171). Another option that is unique is to come down the trail from the top of the cliff by mule. It's not for those afraid of heights. A trip can be arranged by calling Molokai Mule Ride at 800-567-7550. *Please note:* No children under 16 are allowed on Kalaupapa.

Unlike the long, thin Molokai, Lanai Island has a more circular shape. For years it has been known as the Pineapple Island because most of its land was used as a Dole plantation. That has changed over the last couple of decades. The pineapples are gone. Two luxurious resorts with golf courses and extravagant homes have replaced them. While Lanai Island is very pleasant to visit, there really is not much to photograph on land.

For a Lanai day trip I recommend going over by boat. You can take the Lanai Ferry (1-800-695-2624, go-lanai.com) over to Manele Bay. This is the least expensive way to get there, and they make several round-trips a day. You can spend the day exploring, swimming, and snorkeling in Manele Bay and the adjacent Hulopoe Bay. Bring a picnic or wander over to the Manele Bay Hotel. Go-Lanai also offers some activity packages.

The other way is to go over on a tour boat. These mainly offer ocean activities along the western shore of the island. There are high cliffs that block the trade winds, so the water here is calm and clear. It's some of the best snorkeling in Hawaii. During whale season you will almost certainly see them. Trilogy is the company that has the most options and best boats (www.sailtrilogy.com, 1-888-225-6284).

Camera Stores

Lighthaus Camera, 415 Dairy Rd., Suite B, Kahului; 808-877-5155, 143 Dickenson St., Suite 102a, Lahaina; 808-661-5155

Maui Digital Imaging, 75 Kupuohi St., Lahaina 808-661-9750

Costco, 540 Haleakala Hwy, Kahalui; 808-877-5248

Maui Dive Shop (underwater camera gear and rentals), www.mauidiveshop.com /Maui-Rentals/camera-video.htm, 1455 S. Kihei Rd., 800-542-3483

Maui Information

Facts, www.maui-info.com/mauifacts.html

General information, www.gohawaii.com/maui

History, www.frommers.com/destinations /maui/0015020044.html

Visitors Bureau, www.visitmaui.com, 800-525-6284

Weather Today, www.hawaiiweathertoday .com/maui.php

Webcams, www.mauigateway.com/~rw/video /video.htm

Maui Recreation

B&B Reviews, www.tripadvisor.com/Hotels-g 29220-Maui_Hawaii-Hotels.html

Dining Guide and Reviews, www.mauimenus online.com/dining-reviews.html

Diving, www.mauidiveshop.com

Event Calendar, www.calendarmaui.com /index.php

Farmers' Markets, www.ediblecommunities .com/hawaiianislands/farmers-markets /farmers-markets.htm

Hiking, www.trails.com/activity.aspx?area =10037#trailid=HGP008-040&lat=20 .7078&lon=-156.252&zoom=10&m =terrain&a=HK

Hotel Reviews, http://travel.latimes.com /destinations/hawaii/maui/clm/hotels/list

Maui Luau Reviews, mauihawaiiluau.com /luau-reviews.php

Maui Tour Reviews, www.tripadvisor.com /Attractions-g29220-Activities-c25-Maui _Hawaii.html

Surfing, www.mauiinformationguide.com /hawaii-surfing.php

Suggested Reading

Maui Trails, Kathy Morey (Wilderness Press, 2003)

Top Maui Restaurants, James Jacobsen (Maui Media, 2009)

Maui, Glenda Bendure and Ned Friary (Lonely Planet, 2009)

Maui: Great Destinations Hawaii, Carol Fowler (Countryman Press, 2008)

Favorites

Keawakapu Beach

Favorite Beaches for Photos
Napili Bay
Kahekili Beach
Keawakapu Beach

Favorite Sunset Spot
Kaanapali Beach
Launiupoko Beach Park
Malu'aka Beach
Wailea Beach

Favorite Sunrise Spot
Koki Beach
Haleakala from Kalahaku Lookout

Favorite Hikes for Photos
Pipiwai Trail
Nakalelele Blowhole
Redwood Trail Poli Poli

Favorite Waterfalls
Wailua Falls
Lower Puohokamoa Falls
The upper falls at Pua'a Ka'a State Park

Favorite Tours for Photos
Trilogy Sailing to Lanai
Atlantis Submarine
Any sunset cruise on a calm day